Antisocial
Behavior

BENJAMIN B. WOLMAN, Ph.D.

Antisocial Behavior

PERSONALITY

DISORDERS

FROM HOSTILITY

TO HOMICIDE

Prometheus Books

59 John Glenn Drive
Amherst, New York 14228-2197

Published 1999 by Prometheus Books

Inquiries should be addressed to
Prometheus Books
59 John Glenn Drive
Amherst, New York 14228–2197
VOICE: 716–691–0133, ext. 207
FAX: 716–564–2711
WWW.PROMETHEUSBOOKS.COM

08 07 06 05 04   6 5 4 3 2

Library of Congress Cataloging-in-Publication Data

Wolman, Benjamin B.
    Antisocial behavior : personality disorders from hostility to homicide /
Benjamin B. Wolman.
        p. cm.
    Includes bibliographical references and index.
    ISBN 1–57392–701–5 (alk. paper)
    1. Deviant behavior. 2. Social problems. 3. Anitsocial personality disorders.
4. Agressiveness (Psychology). I. Title.

HM811.W65 1999
302.5'42—dc21

                                                          99–26284

Printed in the United States of America on acid-free paper

Contents

8 CONTENTS

Preface

This book is an alarm signal. It was written to *all* people in the United States and other countries. We are concerned with the future of civilization and with the future of moral values created by religion, science, and art. We worry about the growing danger of antisocial behavior. We worry about the future of children who are exposed to violence and are growing up in a climate of excessive permissiveness and passivity.

We are calling on concerned men and women: Wake up! The spread of antisocial, sociopathic behavior is a threat to all of us!

This book has eight chapters. The first chapter reviews the present situation. The second and third chapters describe sociopaths as adults, children, and adolescents. The fourth chapter analyzes the causes of the rise of sociopathic personalities. The fifth chapter offers a historical, cross-cultural analysis of sociopathic behavior. The sixth and seventh

11

chapters suggest ways to combat sociopathy, to stop its spread, and to prevent the epidemic. Our public opinion, the mass media, and the educational system must undergo radical changes. It is our moral responsibility to defend our democratic way of life, cleanse our life of disunity, and cleanse our streets of crime.

I hope that men and women everywhere will follow my message and do the job.

Benjamin B. Wolman

1

The
Present
Situation

The Facts

We are witnessing two dangerous phenomena: On the one hand there is a growing incidence of sociopathic antisocial behavior, and on the other hand an increasing lack of concern coupled with an attitude of moral apathy. And here are the facts.

In 1963 the Federal Bureau of Investigation reported 2,180 crimes per 100,000 population. Thirty years later law-enforcement agencies reported that crime had more than doubled to 5,463 cases per 100,000 population.

On January 30, 1995, *Time* reported that according to a *Time*/CNN survey, 89 percent of those surveyed said that the crime situation in the United States is getting worse, and 55 percent were afraid that they would become victims themselves.

According to Janet Reno, the attorney general, "Never in our history have we seen this phenomenon of youth violence as random and as inexplicable."[1] From 1968 to 1993 the number of arrests of juveniles rose by 68 percent.

On April 19, 1995, a terrorist bomb murdered 168 innocent men, women, and children. The bomb destroyed the Alfred P. Murrah Federal Building in Oklahoma City, burying many and killing nineteen children, causing serious wounds to many adults and children.

A few days earlier G. Gordon Liddy, the Watergate conspirator who hosts the second most widely heard radio talk show, advised his listeners to shoot federal agents.

According to *U.S. News & World Report*: "The time has focused attention on the militia or, as it is also called, patriot movement and its potential for violence. Most of those who join the paramilitary units—some of which offer training with high-powered weaponry—do so because they expect one day to have to defend themselves against a government or United Nations onslaught envisioning a new world order." A picture on the very same page shows neo-nazis demonstrating near New Hope, Pennsylvania, "wearing Confederate flags, a swastika and a modern German flag."[2] The Center for Democratic Renewal, which monitors the militias, estimates that there are "up to 100,000 members in at least thirty states, *most of whom have enlisted in the past two years*" (emphasis added). The Christian Identity movement holds that while Europeans are God's chosen people, Jews are children of Satan and blacks and Asians are animalistic mud.

Time reported that Timothy McVeigh, at the time the

chief suspect in the Oklahoma City bombing, wrote in 1992 to the editors of the *Union-Sun & Journal*: "Do we have to shed blood to reform the current system? I hope it doesn't come to that. But it might."[3]

The cases of terrorism clearly indicate the need to wake up, and the recent nerve gas attack in Tokyo and the mass murder of men, women, and children in Oklahoma are alarm signals. Due to technological advances, the terrorists may get control of atomic weapons and put an end to humankind as we know it.

According to the book *Final Warning: Averting Disaster in the New Age of Terrorism*, terrorist organizations are crossing historic thresholds of violence with the help of increasingly sophisticated technology: "In the 1980s missiles have become more sophisticated and much more available."[4] In 1984 these organizations predicted that "Future terrorist attacks will inflict high numbers of casualties . . . [and] will cause widespread fear."[5] "A new age of terrorism is arriving, heralded by an act of breathtaking terror."[6]

"Most terrorist gangs will continue to employ the usual weapons, machine guns, rockets, and bombs, etc. Some groups however, are becoming technically more adept. . . . The consequences of miscalculating a sophisticated terrorist intention are absolutely frightening."[7]

Imagine that a terrorist group takes over a community and believes they have the right to do as they please. Imagine a stockpile of nuclear weapons within their grasp. Are we the crazy ones, we the peaceful and law-abiding citizens, who ignore the problem and calm ourselves by ignoring the danger?

Terrorism is a grave sociopolitical and psychological problem that requires a thorough and responsible analysis. The roots of contemporary terrorism are associated with the two great terrorist systems of Hitler and Stalin, and a sober look into the dynamics of terror may be of help in the urgent task of stopping the epidemic of sociopathy. The goal of the Nazi movement was mass murder of all "inferior races" starting with the Jews, and world domination by the German *Herrenvolk* (nation of lords). Dictatorial systems believe *that the end justifies the means, and they have the right to impose their will on the rest of humankind.* They believe they have the right to put people in concentration camps and gas chambers or in the Gulag Archipelago. They believe they, and only they, have the right to kidnap, torture, and murder. In the name of what they believe in, they have the right to do as they please.

This philosophy has been practiced by Idi Amin, Ayatollah Khomeini, Jim Jones, and Muammar Qaddafi, among others. This is the *raison d'être* of the Red Brigades, Baader-Meinhof gang, the Palestine Liberation Organization (PLO), Irish Republican Army (IRA), Basque Fatherland and Liberty (ETA), and the United States paramilitary anti-American groups.

Undoubtedly, dictatorial ideas and their terrorist offshoots attract some people for the following reasons: (1) They set a goal, a purpose, a task to be fulfilled. They offer their followers a meaning to their lives and thus counteract the existential nihilism of our times. (2) They give their members a feeling of superiority (Raskolnikov's elitism) and enable them to look down on the rest of humanity, believing that only they have the wisdom and the courage to act in a bold and reckless way while serving some allegedly sublime goal. (3) Acting in a group and following an inspiring leader or an idea obliterates the normal feelings of fear and guilt and thus (4) enables otherwise normal individuals to practice self-righteous violence. And last, but perhaps the most important reason, (5) their actions are usually successful. *They give their participants the glorious feelings of achievement and victory; they do get away with murder.*

"On April 18, 1983, a delivery van filled with explosives was driven to the front of the U.S. Embassy in Beirut. When it detonated, it flattened most of the building, killing seventeen Americans and forty-six others. The Reagan administration learned that Syria had been involved, but Iran had ordered the attack."[8]

"Terrorists are often supplied with guns and explosives that are brought into victim nations under the eyes of customs officers who are forbidden by international law to open any shipment that arrives under the protection of a diplomatic seal. The 'diplomatic pouch' as it is known, is one of the most critical pieces of terrorist infrastructure."[9]

As early as 1967 in the *George Washington Law Review* FBI director J. Edgar Hoover wrote on "Violence in American Society—A Problem of Critical Concern." "Over the years, America's constitutional system has been one of its most noble accomplishments. Wisely, the Founding Fathers understood the true inner nature of man; they realized that a system of government based on law subject to change by the consent of the governed was man's best protection against himself." But today, "The psychology of lawlessness is reflected in myriad ways in our society. For example, there are crimes of violence . . . gang fights, underworld crime, and forcible rapes form part of the picture of violence—often abetted by lax procedures of judicial leniency. . . ."[10]

Apparently the vast majority of people in the United States seem to be aware of the sociopathic epidemic and the spiral of violence, but not ready to cope with the danger. The rise of sociopathy represents a grave danger to civilization and to the democratic way of life. Democratic societies allow the same degree of freedom to *all* members. People care but they do next to nothing.

Human life is interaction, and human beings depend on each other. The growing incidence of sociopathic behavior implies dangerous regression. A tree cannot go back and become a seedling or a seed, and it may become a crippled tree. The survival of our civilized and democratic way of life is the responsibility of all of us.

Self-Defeating Liberals

A society that does not have strict moral standards backed up by consistent mass media, a society that tolerates unethical behavior, or a society that does not offer persistent protection to peaceful citizens, creates an ideal environment for sociopaths and encourages antisocial behavior. The permissive attitude toward unfair and dishonest practices in business and in public life, where public opinion, movies, and television, wittingly or unwittingly, glorify the "tough guy," provides the fertile soil for a rise in sociopathic behavior.

Social relationships and social organizations are based on renunciation of the individual's unlimited freedom of action. If this renunciation is voluntary and agreed upon by the participants, it serves as a basis for democracy. Undoubtedly such self-restraint by agreement is beneficial to all parties concerned, for it promises *the same degree of freedom for all*. However, human history is full of individuals who demanded *all freedom for themselves and no freedom for others*. These individuals have tried, often successfully, to impose their will on others, and have spread violence and chaos.

It seems that the present-day sociopsychological climate fosters antisocial behavior, which with the proliferation and improvements in weaponry, may mean mass suicide. The two world wars and a host of lesser wars did not cool our aggressive appetites, and the inclination to violent behavior seems to take on epidemic dimensions both in international relations and also within the boundaries of practically every country.

Former Atlanta Police Chief Napper said, "There are a lot of young guys who just don't care, who go out and blow people away just for the hell of it."[11] Darryl Gates, the former chief of the Los Angeles Police, said, "We have lost a whole generation. No self-discipline. Total indulgence. Drugs. Lack of respect for the law. Lack of respect for values. A whole generation thumbed its nose at everything that was held sacred in this country. America has to take a look at its heart and soul."[12] According to B. K. Johnson, Houston

Police Chief, "We have allowed ourselves to degenerate to the point where we are living like animals. We live behind burglar bars and throw a collection of door locks at night. Today many people seek escape in hedonism [have fun] and pseudo-liberalism [let them do whatever they like to do]."

The way Lenin and later Hitler conquered their countries should serve as a lesson for all of us, but unfortunately, humanity has rarely if ever learned from past errors. John Reed's book *Ten Days that Shook the World*, while friendly to the Bolsheviks, describes their reckless attacks on the shaky democratic system of Kerensky. William Shirer's *The Rise and Fall of the Third Reich* pointed to the ruthless savagery of the Nazis and the inept and helpless German democracy.

In both cases the *appalling permissiveness* of the liberal governments *encouraged* the future dictators and *enabled* them to destroy the democratic system. *Weakness invites aggression*, but in both cases it was not real weakness. Kerensky had enough power to defend the budding Russian democracy and the German liberals of the Weimar Republic could have squelched Nazism instead of allowing the Nazis to arm themselves and become a powerful military organization. Both the Russian and German liberals practiced suicidal helplessness and their weakness was self-imposed. Instead of defending democracy, they surrendered it to the dictators.

The appallingly helpless liberals discouraged and alienated many of their followers, while the determined and aggressive tyrants gained plenty of public support. Weak people lose their friends. Strong people attract them. The self-imposed weakness was suicidal. Whoever allows people to get away with murder, invites murder.

I am under the impression that the *law-abiding and peaceloving citizens in democratic countries encourage terrorism and are guilty of the proliferation of self-righteous violence.*

The proliferation of violent behavior has little if anything to do with rational causes. Catholics and protestants in Northern Ireland could have solved their differences without killing each other. No one attacks radical groups in Italy or Israel or any other place. Peaceful Germans today are better off now than they were during Hitler's robberies, and Belgians are not worse off after they lost the Congo. Moreover, neither the PLO nor the IRA nor the ETA have any chance to win, and they know it. Sociopolitical conflicts can be solved only by negotiations. Terrorism solves none; it is futile, but it mushrooms wherever it is allowed to flourish. Those good-natured and well-wishing people who support the IRA, who advocate public recognition of violent groups, who sympathize with the ETA in Spain or Baader-Meinhof in Germany or Red Brigades in Italy or any other terrorists *unwillingly and unwittingly undermine the ramparts of our civilized and democratic way of life.*

The problem is not with the poor souls who kill for kicks or for glory, uttering high-sounding slogans. The problem is with us, men and women *who can and should defend themselves by total disapproval, by unanimous condemnation, and, whenever necessary, by force.* Two hundred years ago the English political thinker Edmund Burke said: "The only thing necessary for the triumph of evil is for good men to do nothing."

Preventive methods must be applied in long-range planning. Something went wrong with our educational system at home and in school. The educational pendulum swung 180 degrees: from blindly obeying parents and teachers to total anarchy at home and a blackboard jungle in schools. Some years ago children were supposed to be seen and not heard; today, in many homes, parents are not heard and hardly seen. A total misunderstanding of democratic principles, combined with gross distortion of the teachings of John Dewey and Sigmund Freud, has created a dangerous state of confusion in many homes.

Animals and infants act in accordance with their phylogenetic and ontogenetic level; the same rule applies to human adults. Acquisition of culture is a part of the phylogenetic evolution, and growth through maturation and learning is a part of the ontogenetic evolution. Normal— that is, well-adjusted—individuals are neither as natural as animals nor as immature as infants. They are *cultured* and *mature*.

The phylogenetic cultural and the ontogenetic individual maturation are intrinsically interlocked with inhibitions. Culture started when wise men imposed the "Thou shalt not" rules. Even primitive people could not live together without imposing restraint and demanding self-restraint on sexual and aggressive impulses. These restraints have become a part of human nature, and mature adults are capable of self-control. Culture and inhibition have become their nature.

Renunciation of cultural norms and self-restraint does not return one to the crib or the jungle. It leads to the mental hospital. Human beings cannot turn the clock back; when they try it, the clock breaks and severe behavior disorders take place.

A tree cannot become a sapling and a sapling cannot become a seed. An adult who regresses to infantile modes of behavior does not become an infant, but a severely disturbed adult. Mental disorder is a failure to grow up.[13]

Disinhibited behavior, similar to severe psychosis, can be found in animals and in human neonates. A retrospective look into the phylogenetic and ontogenetic aspects of human evolution discovers the roots of psychosis. Judging by comparative-evolutionary standards, psychotic behavior is *regressive*; in other words, it is as "natural" as the behavior of animals, and it resembles the early infantile modes of behavior. When all ego and superego inhibitions are removed, individuals do not exercise control over their bowels and bladder; they do not practice any sort of self-restraint; they bite when hungry; they rape or masturbate when sexually aroused; they attack when annoyed—in short, their "spontaneous" behavior knows no limits.

A story has been told about an anthropologist who asked the director of a mental hospital to allow him to spend some time on a ward for a research project. He wished to be admitted as if he were a mental patient, and remain in this role undiscovered until the end of his study; he asked the psychiatrist's recommendation. The psychiatrist's advice was simple: "Be yourself and act naturally."

And here is an estimate of the present-day moral standards: We are living in an era of violence. Corrupt politics makes a mockery of moral platitudes. Old fears of breaking the moral laws are gone. As long as prominent offenders consistently escape prosecution, and politicians pal with corrupt elements, we cannot decry the delinquencies of the young. We fail to present our youth with a consistent, morally wholesome set of values. This is the one basic reason why preaching to the young is often greeted by them with cynicism.

Notes

1. *Time*, January 30, 1995.
2. *U.S. News & World Report*, May 8, 1995, p. 37.
3. *Time*, May 8, 1995.
4. Robert H. Kupperman and Jeff Kamen, *Final Warning: Averting Disaster in the New Age of Terrorism* (New York: Doubleday, 1989), p. 9.
5. Ibid., p. 193.
6. Ibid., p. 19.
7. Ibid., p. 116.
8. Ibid., p. 7.
9. Ibid., p. 17.
10. *George Washington Law Review*.
11. *Time*, March 21, 1981.
12. Ibid.
13. Benjamin B. Wolman, *Call No Man Normal* (New York: International Universities Press, 1973).

2

Sociopathic Adults

I was teaching in a postdoctoral program in a medical college and supervised residents in psychiatry. One day a resident whom I supervised was called to the emergency room in the hospital to talk to a young man who tried to kill his wife. I went with the resident.

The young man greeted us and spoke in a friendly and cheerful manner. He was married to a rich young woman and in a few months she had a baby. He was very nice to his wife because her wealthy parents promised to finance him when he started a new business. "But, as you doctors know," he said, "one cannot trust anybody." And he still had to hold on to his old job. He resented his in-laws and he grew impatient with his "selfish wife" and the baby. He decided to kill them and let them "go to hell," but two weeks earlier they had moved out and joined the in-laws in their cooperative apartment across the street.

What follows are the events of that day: He didn't feel

well and didn't go to work. He went out to lunch and came back to his apartment. He found his wife invading *his* apartment and snooping in *his* desk. "I am looking for the baby's birth certificate," she said. "It must be in the desk."

He yelled at her: "What right do you have to come to *my* home?! I'll teach you a lesson!" He went to the kitchen, picked up the heaviest hammer, and "tapped" her on the head. She fell down bleeding on the floor. Then he went to the phone and called for an ambulance.

He turned to me and the resident psychiatrist. "Don't you think, doctors," he asked smiling, "that I was right? Wouldn't you do the same? And I myself called for an ambulance! Wasn't I nice to that bitch? What right did she have to snoop in *my* desk?!"

He was absolutely sure that his behavior was proof of his moral standards. He kept explaining to me and to the resident that he broke with his wife "because she did not serve her husband." He didn't want to have a child, but "isn't a child a woman's responsibility?" His wife had the nerve to ask him to help her with the baby.

But this wasn't everything! He married her because she had very wealthy parents who promised to help him start his own business, but they did not keep their promise! The father-in-law was a liar! He told the son-in-law that he would give him money, but he only gave him an advance! He still owed some money.

The young man turned to the resident: "Would you stay married to a selfish woman with her procrastinating father? Wouldn't you prefer to be free? Am I responsible for her and for the baby?"

She moved out to her parents' apartment across the street. Her mother hired a full-time baby nurse. "These people are rich and selfish pigs! Why did she keep the keys to *my* apartment? What right did she have to look in *my* desk? Didn't I have the right to teach her a lesson? Don't people have the right to protect their property? I just tapped her stupid head with a hammer! And when she fell on the floor *I* called for an ambulance. *I* called, *I* helped, all *I*. Wasn't *I* nice to her?"

Clinical Practice

This story is not unique. The cases of selfish behavior repeat themselves more often than ever before. It looks as if a spreading of antisocial behavior has become an epidemic. More and more people care for no one except themselves. More and more people have no moral commitments. There are more people who don't trust anyone and believe that they are always right, no matter what they do.

Many psychiatrists, psychologists, and clinical social workers say the same thing. They say that the incidence of antisocial behavior is growing rapidly. More and more people don't care for anyone except themselves.

Not only do clinicians say so, but every day the mass media report new cases of selfishness, deceit, fraud, burglary, rape, and murder. Are these people aware of what they are doing? Apparently they feel that they have the right to do as they please. No feelings of remorse, no sense of guilt—an epidemic of sociopaths. In Freud's time hysteria was the most frequent mental problem; today sociopathy is most frequent!

The *Diagnostic and Statistical Manual of Mental Disorders,* third edition revised, defines sociopathy as follows:

Antisocial Personality Disorder

The essential feature of this disorder is a pattern of irresponsible and antisocial behavior beginning in childhood or early adolescence and continuing into adulthood. For this diagnosis to be given, the person must be at least eighteen years of age and have a history of Conduct Disorder before the age of fifteen.

Lying, stealing, truancy, vandalism, initiating fights, running away from home, and physical cruelty are typical childhood signs. In adulthood the antisocial pattern continues, and may include failure to honor financial obligations, to function as a responsible parent or to plan ahead, and an inability to sustain consistent work behavior. These people fail to conform to social norms and repeatedly perform antisocial acts that are grounds for arrest, such as destroying property, harassing others, stealing, and having an illegal occupation.

People with Antisocial Personality Disorder tend to be irritable and aggressive and to repeatedly get into physical fights and assaults, including spouse- or child-beating. Reckless behavior without regard to personal safety is common, as indicated by frequently driving while intoxicated or getting speeding tickets. Typically, these people are promiscuous (defined as never having sustained a monogamous relationship for more than a year). Finally, they generally have no remorse about the effects of their behavior on others; they may even feel justified in having hurt or mistreated others. After age thirty, the more flagrantly antisocial behavior may diminish, particularly sexual promiscuity, fighting, and criminality.[1]

Sociopaths do believe that their actions are *always justified* and that they have the right to use force to get whatever they want. A thirty-five-year-old married businessman complained about his wife: Does marriage imply chastity? Must a married man become a slave to his wife? Does marriage mean renunciation of one's sexual freedom, civil rights, and personal relationships? Isn't a wife a selfish person who demands attention and affection?

He continued: Whenever she would follow him in the evening going on a date, he pushed her away. He never hurt her; he believed that he was always a gentle, kind, concerned person! But he had to defend his personal freedom, and if his pushing hurt her, it was her own fault!

Sociopathic Behavior

Sociopaths operate on the premise that friends should be used and adversaries destroyed. They believe in their innocence. They are aggressive to those who fear them, and obedient and subservient to those they fear. In milder cases they appear as selfish individuals; in severe cases they are cruel criminals. They may torture and mutilate their victims and their cruelty enhances their feeling of power.

They believe that they are innocent victims of injustice and they have the right to defend themselves against a cold and hostile world. Sociopaths maintain that their victims are guilty, and they must fight them in self-defense. Quite often they believe that they are entitled to material gains at the expense of other people. Some of them use force for self-aggrandizement or, as they explain it, "for kicks." They often develop paranoid fears and suspect that they are being watched or persecuted. However, when undisturbed in their criminal activities or when the victims show cooperation, they may abstain from violence. They act as if saying: "As long as the world recognizes my rights to them, I shall control my impulses. But when the world becomes a threat by denying me my rights, I will not control myself and my impulses will break loose."

Not all antisocial behavior is a product of sociopathic personality structure. Antisocial and aggressive behavior can be caused by a variety of organic, social, and psychological factors.

Adjustment to one's society is one of the most important determinants of mental health. Society cannot tolerate unrestricted aggression. Civilized societies permit the use of force in self-defense only, and this only in a way prescribed by their legal systems. Well-adjusted individuals keep their hostile impulses under rational control. Whether they compete or cooperate, love or hate, they are not carried away by their impulses. They are neither saints nor sinners. They are not afraid to bear hostility against those who hurt them and they defend their rights within socially approved limits.

A sociopath is a narcissistic person who has no sense of responsibility, lacks self-control, and is antisocial. Sociopaths lack insight and compassion; they are unable to assume responsibility, to accept blame, to feel guilty, and to have concern for anyone.

Two patterns of social interaction can be distinguished. The imbalance between or distortion of these patterns constitutes mental disorder. First, there is the *instrumental* social pattern, of which the infant-toward-parent interaction is the prototype. In this pattern, the individual is a *taker* and uses others to satisfy his own needs. In normal life, child-parent and business relationships are instrumental. However, the instrumental pattern of relating may become distorted and a *hyperinstrumental* sociopathic pattern of behavior emerges.

Some mentally disturbed individuals are hyperinstrumental. They always want something for nothing; they show no consideration for their fellow human being, not even for their own parents, marital partners, or children; they act convinced that the world owes them a living, but they don't owe anything to anyone in return. They have no love for anyone except themselves. They are exploitive, selfish, brutal to others, and sentimental toward themselves. They feel sorry for themselves but have no mercy for anyone else. They never blame themselves, but always blame others. They believe themselves to be weak and friendly, surrounded by selfish and unfair enemies.

Violent Sociopaths

There are three types of sociopaths: (1) violent, (2) charming, and (3) passive.

Violence is older than humanity itself, and human beings have been engaged in intraspecific, intragroup, and fratricidal wars. Living together offers numerous opportunities for cooperation, and intraspecific cooperation increases the chances for survival of the members of the group. In many instances, herbivorous animals form a defensive circle against predatory beasts. On the other hand, a pack of wolves has a better chance of killing a deer than a single wolf.

Human beings often outdo animals. As soon as the persecution of Christians in Rome came to an end, the Christians began to persecute others. The "great" French revolutionaries who rebelled against King Louis XVI's tyranny sent to death not only enemies but also their most ardent supporters, the Hebertists. The victorious Russian Communists, as soon as they defeated the counterrevolutionary "White" armies, attacked the anarchists and the left wing Social Revolutionaries who had helped them in the October 1917 Revolution. After Lenin's death his disciples engaged for decades in mass murder of their past comrades.

People who feel secure, that is, who have a high estimate of their power, don't have the need to abuse it. People who doubt their power may be inclined to assert themselves and tend to act aggressively. Hostile behavior, whether offensive or defensive, is not necessarily maladjustive, as long as it serves self-protection and survival. It becomes maladjusted when there is no real threat or when the estimation of the threat is grossly exaggerated.

The feeling of weakness and helplessness makes people hate whoever they could blame for their failures. Some people tend to overestimate the power of others and thus misconstrue their intentions, and fear hostility where no hostile action is intended against them.

Insecure people admire "heroes" and wish to imitate them. It has always been easier to destroy than to build. Destruction requires little effort, endurance, and courage. Many children brought up by immature and wishy-washy parents learn to extort concessions by temper tantrums. Insecure parents who fear growing old often try to prevent the growth of their children. Sometimes they prefer to see them taking dope, playing "free" sex, and making "revolutions" rather than becoming responsible individuals.

The weaker one is, the more secure one feels in a mob. It is always easier to *fight* for peace, religion, social justice, and all the good slogans than to *work* for them. Violence and *destruction* give one the much yearned for *illusion of power*, while creative efforts make one aware of the limitations of one's power. Roaming mobs give one the feeling of power. Feelings of inferiority can easily be overcompensated by violence. The fact that one needs little power for destructive actions makes violence attractive to sociopaths torn by feelings of inadequacy and inferiority.

All living organisms carry a certain amount of energy that becomes activated by a threat to life. The built-in release-apparatus, the force that opens the valves of the hydraulic model, is called *instinctual drive*. It starts as *Ares*, the symbol of fighting and war, and its energy is called *destrudo*. At a certain evolutionary level, part of this energy became invested in procreation, or the preservation of the life of the species, as if the life of one individual continued through its offspring. This is *Eros* and its energy is called *libido*.

As long as an organism is alive, its energies can either be directed toward the promotion of life or toward its destruction. The innate, instinctual force, "lust for life," is divided into two arms: the one that serves promotion of life is *Eros*, or love. Love can be directed toward oneself or toward others. The other arm serves destruction and is called *Ares*. Ares, too, can be directed toward oneself or toward others. Life and death deal with *quantities* of energy. The instincts of love and hostility deal with the *direction* in which the mental energy, respectively libido and destrudo, is used.

Ares starts in infancy as a defense against dangers, combined with self-directed, narcissistic Eros. Ares may become hate without danger and cruelty without gain, or cruelty combined with sexual pleasure, or hate for oneself. Consider the Vandals; after looting the classic treasures of Rome, they demolished whatever they could not carry away with them. During the Second World War the Germans plundered, tortured, and murdered with and without reasons. Destrudo can be acted out for the sheer pleasure of vandalism.

The history of persecutions and wars, especially the history of Nazi Germany, bear unmistakable witness to the brutal force of Ares. Although Ares starts as a self-defensive device, in sociopathic people it becomes a goal in itself. The discharge of destructive energy creates a feeling of power, and hitting someone makes one feel strong and enhances the faith in one's own vitality.

Apparently, there are no developmental phases in Ares. Libido, however, goes through developmental phases such as the oral and the phallic, but destrudo remains always the same—a primordial, primitive, destructive drive that cannot be eradicated or cured. It can only be restrained. Sociopaths retain their hostile attitude as long as they are alive.

There are two main sources of violence, namely *the fear of death by starvation* and *the fear of death by being killed.* The fear of having nothing to eat leads to *offensive violence*, and the fear of being eaten leads to *defensive violence*. To eat and not to be eaten, this is the goal.

Animal violence is usually interspecific: the predators practice *offensive violence* and their victims practice *defensive violence* to prevent being eaten. Intraspecific violence is usually related to a fight with an animal group for access to food, water, and sex. Most often intraspecific fights are not murderous, and the intraspecific competition is usually settled by establishing a pecking order. However, in several species the intraspecific violence is murderous. Hippopotamus, deer, musk, human beings, and some other species kill in intraspecific violence.

Only human beings are painfully aware of the inevitable end, and are therefore more eager to fight. Being capable of or anticipating and/or imagining future dangers, they are almost always ready to fight offensive and defensive wars.

The fear of death by starvation and the fear of being killed are the main causes of human belligerence. The fear of not having food motivates hatred toward those who have plenty: the underprivileged, poor, and hungry human beings tend to resent the wealthy ones. The fear of being harmed, enslaved, and/or killed motivates hatred toward the powerful whether they are true or imaginary enemies.

People hate powerful and potentially dangerous adversaries. The feeling of *insecurity* is a frequent cause of hatred and violent behavior. Usually people do not fear or hate poor and weak relatives, but they envy and often hate their rich and powerful ones.

Power

Survival is the chief motivation of human behavior. Survival depends on one's power, that is, one's ability to obtain food and shelter, and to defend oneself against enemies. Power can be defined as the ability to satisfy one's own needs and the needs of others, as well as the ability to prevent the satisfaction of the needs of others. Preventing one's own needs, such as self-imposed starvation, martyrdom, and suicide, do not belong to the category of power.

Elation and depression originate in true or exaggerated feelings of strength and weakness. People are elated when they feel powerful, and they are depressed when they feel weak and powerless. Elation carries the message of power; depression is a psychological corollary of feeling weak and angry at oneself for being weak.

Violent behavior can give people the illusion of power. One bomb can destroy a house that was built by many. It takes years of tender love and care to bring up a child, but one terrorist can kill many children. It takes plenty of power to create, but it does not take much power to destroy. Small wonder then that many young people and adults are easy prey for fanatics and gang leaders. Mussolini's fascist "arditi," Hitler's SS and SA gangs, Stalin's and Jagoda's henchmen, the IRA, the PLO, and other terrorists feel empowered when they kill innocent people.

There is a magnetic attraction in terrorist gangs. Joining a dictatorial cult or a terrorist gang suspends individual responsibility, obliterates guilt feelings, and removes moral inhibitions. Some people tend to assault, mug, or kill, but it has always been easy to incite *average* people to a robbery, to a pogrom of Jews, to lynching of blacks, and to kidnapping of American businessmen and diplomats. The main attractiveness of violent behavior is the psychological attractiveness of *power*.

The Proliferation of Violence

The proliferation of drug abuse and violent crime is a dangerous sign of cultural regression. Civilization started when social rules of behavior—"Thou shalt not"—were imposed. The decline in self-discipline and the increase in disinhibition are dangerous signs of deculturation, reminding us what happens when social rules are permitted to lapse.

The present-day social climate of excessive hedonism and the widely spread "have-fun" attitudes encourage alcoholism and drug abuse and the "do-whatever-pleases-you" mentality. This selfish, hedonistic social climate fosters the sociopathic personality.

Every day we read or hear about someone being mugged, raped, or killed. Shoplifting and burglaries are matched by extortion, dope pushing, and holdups. So far, nothing has stopped crime, and antisocial and antihuman acts go on seemingly unchecked. The judicial and penal systems are apparently unable to put an end to the spread of criminal behavior. Jailing lawbreakers was never an adequate deterrent, and in many instances penitentiaries have turned out hardened criminals who are more vicious and more determined than ever before. Leniency and permissiveness did not fare better, and the soft system of justice has often given the impression that, indeed, one can "get away with murder."

Several factors contribute to the increase in violence, among them the *abundance of lethal weapons and the apparent weakness in control of violence*. Criminals armed with automatic weapons can attack anybody and everybody, and courts and police are often inadequate in protecting innocent citizens. At the present time violent people usually can get away with murder.

Violent gangs have an easy time, and their easy success is quite apparent in the fight against terrorism. Terrorist groups are more numerous and better armed than ever, and so far there is no end to terrorism. Moreover, the U.S. Task Force on Nuclear Terrorism concluded in 1987 that building a crude nuclear device is well within the reach of a terrorist group that can recruit a few specialists. The team need not even have prior experience in weapons design but would only require chemical high explosives, which are easy to obtain, and a sufficient quantity of fissionable nuclear materials.

Designing an atomic weapon is not as difficult a task as it was in the past. Enterprising students at MIT, Harvard, and Princeton have independently "designed weapons" on paper. A student-led course in nuclear-weapons design was proposed, but not given, at the University of Connecticut. To the physicist, the most important piece of information about atomic devices was learned at Alamogordo, New Mexico, in 1944: supercritical masses of fissionable materials explode. Criminals motivated by greed, or terrorists seeking political power, need only build a crude device that will explode.

Charming Sociopaths

Sociopaths are exceedingly selfish, overdemanding, manipulative, and exploitive, and none of them has any remorse or guilt feelings. Sociopaths tend to lie, cheat, take advantage, and exploit, and they always find some way to justify their behavior. They never blame themselves and they harbor paranoid suspicions and accusations of others. They believe that they are "innocent victims" of adverse conditions and/or hostile environments, and they justify their hostile actions by the need to defend themselves.

Sociopaths try to win attention and present themselves as victims of "unfair treatment" and of "lack of luck." They harbor infantile attitudes and expect others to take care of them.

A thirty-two-year-old man who was hired as an executive in his in-laws' flourishing business, was coming to the office in the morning for two or three hours and stealing cash. He usually lunched with one of his girlfriends, and spent the afternoons in a luxurious apartment he purchased with the money stolen from his in-laws. After all, he said, he was a young man and he believed that he had the right to enjoy himself.

When his wife became pregnant, he told her that he must go out of town to meet with his customers. He left New York with one of his girlfriends and charged the trip to the business as a "necessary business expense." He explained to me that men never get pregnant, and there is no reason for a man to become a baby-sitter for his pregnant wife. He was always nice to her, taking her out to luxurious restaurants (of course, at business expense). Apparently her pregnancy was unusually difficult and he intended to call her on his trip. She could call her doctor and even have a nurse on hand, but there was no reason for him to stay home with her. And if there were a miscarriage, no one could blame him.

Charming sociopaths do not care for anyone, but tend to act in a friendly manner. The young man was coming to my office before he became a hypochondriac, and hoped for assurance and emotional support. As mentioned before, I call sociopaths *narcissistic hyperinstrumentals*, because all they want is to receive. They expect instant gratification of their needs and they exercise very little, if any, self-criticism. They are self-centered; preoccupied with sensuous pleasures; and are prone to sexual promiscuity, perversion, and alcohol and drug abuse. They get angry when confronted with a difficult task and usually expect special privileges. They tend to be negligent and dishonest on their jobs, and get angry when their superiors present them with a job that requires effort. They perceive demands as an imposition, and try to evade difficulty by cheating or by rebellion, depending on the estimate of the adversary's strength.

Perceptual distortions are frequent occurrences in childhoods of these charming sociopaths, and memory defects may develop at any age. Observational errors and unrealistic reports may happen to many but they are not lies as long as they are not intentional.

Lying is an *intentionally* misleading form of communication. People may lie occasionally, but sociopaths lie on every possible occasion, and feel no regrets, no remorse, and no guilt. Sociopaths lie consciously and intentionally in order to enable them to take advantage of other people. Sociopaths are deliberate liars who use lying for deceiving and cheating, and always for their own gain.

My sociopathic patients are convinced that everybody else is a liar. They cannot believe that there are people who tell the truth and even feel guilty when they tell a lie. My sociopathic patients assure me that people who deny their lies are compulsive liars. On a few occasions charming sociopathic patients assured me, always in a polite and friendly manner, that I was an "old-fashioned moralist."

Not all alcoholics are sociopaths and not all sociopaths are alcoholics, but there is a high correlation between sociopathy and alcoholism. Temporary alcoholic intoxication of a nonalcoholic may lead to irresponsible behavior, but sociopaths do not need alcohol since they tend to exhibit antisocial behavior when they are sober.

Quite often their antisocial actions are calculated and directed toward some sort of gain. Charming sociopaths do not fight against powerful adversaries; they are looking for a nonaggressive sure victory. Most sociopaths prefer to seduce children rather than adults, for children cannot defend themselves. Most rape cases of old and helpless women are committed by sociopaths, for a "friendly rape" gives them a double pleasure of sex and power. They are criticized for unfair strategies and untruthful promises; they lie and maintain that *they* would never lie, and the woman who blames them is always the seductive person.

Alcohol abuse and antisocial behavior usually starts in the person's early teens. Early alcoholism is often associated with other patterns of antisocial behavior, such as truancy, disobedience, disrespect for teachers, extorting money from schoolmates, running away from home, and joining criminal gangs. Today more often than ever before, sociopathic alcoholics gang up on a lonely girl and rape her. One of my female patients was raped by a gang of her classmates when she was in high school; all of them were heavy drinkers.

As the sociopathic alcoholic grows up, he or she becomes more abusive toward peers and parents. Sociopaths always maintain that their victims "provoked" them and "started the fight." One young man in college told me that he could have "broken his father's arm," but, of course, "he was very considerate." When his father accused him of being a "bum and an alcoholic," he merely hit his father once and "threw him on the floor," though his father "deserved a more severe punishment."

Drug dependence is not limited to sociopaths and not all sociopaths are drug addicts, but many sociopaths are drug users and many drug users turn out to be sociopaths.

Sociopaths are notorious pleasure seekers and exercise poor, if any, self-control. When they are forced to undergo institutional treatment, they tend to justify their behavior and to blame everyone else for their addiction.

Passive Sociopaths

Passive sociopaths are not aggressive individuals. They do not hate or actively assault others. They do not care for anyone except themselves, and would not go out of their way to help, care for, or save another. When they see someone drowning (and they happen to be good swimmers) they would not try to save the drowning person. Most probably they would continue doing whatever they were doing, and wouldn't bother to call for help. In the event of an accident on the street they would simply drive away. When their own child is sick, they may try to get rid of the sick child. Some have been known to divorce a sick spouse instead of caring for the person. It is just *me, me, me,* and no one else who must be taken care of.

Over the years I have had in therapy gravely depressed people who contemplated suicide. My strategy with suicidal patients is clearly determined at the beginning of therapy. I always tell them the following:

"You came to me for help. You wouldn't ask me to help you if you didn't have faith in me, and you trust me 100 percent. Psychotherapy is a two-way street. It is interaction between two individuals who trust one another. Psychotherapy is interaction and genuine cooperation.

"These are my terms: I promise to do everything I can to help you, provided you will give me your word of honor that whenever you have suicidal thoughts, you will call me. I will see you as soon as I can, and I have your word of honor that you will not do anything until you come to my office and I can talk to you."

I never failed with this approach, and I have no human life on my conscience. I practiced psychotherapy for over forty years, during which I had in my office several suicidal patients, and I helped each of them. Sociopaths, by the way, are not suicidal; they would rather kill someone else than themselves.

A few years ago I had in psychotherapy a severely depressed young man. He blamed himself for alleged sins that he never committed. He had deep feelings of inferiority, and did not believe that he had the right to live. He was profoundly suicidal.

I told him that if he wanted me to help him, he must help me to help him. I couldn't accept him as my patient unless he would cooperate with me and give me his word of honor to see me whenever he felt suicidal. If I were out of town, he would have to wait for me. He agreed and we started therapy.

I usually call my office frequently to check for messages. Once, at eleven o'clock in the evening, when I was at a meeting, I called my office. There was a message from the doorman. "Dr. Wolman," the doorman pleaded. "A young man came in. He sits in the lobby and cries. He came here an hour ago. Please come!" What else could I do? I took a cab to my office. The twenty-two-year-old man sat there crying.

"I am so glad that you came," he said. "I promised to call you whenever I feel like killing myself. I am very depressed. Please talk to me. I don't know what to do. I feel like killing myself."

I invited him to come into my office. I knew quite well that he was greatly depressed. Something very bad must have happened to him. He needed help desperately. We talked and talked for two hours. I managed to calm him down, then called a cab and had the driver take him to his apartment.

As soon as I came home I called my client's father who lived just two blocks from the patient.

"Dr. Wolman, do you know what time it is now?" the father asked in an angry voice. I answered: "It is almost 2:00 A.M. I left Jim twenty minutes ago. Could you go over and stay with him for a while?" The father hung up on me.

Not all selfish people are inclined to hurt others. They are totally involved with themselves and simply don't care for anyone else. They would not go out of their way to cause harm to other people, but neither would they go out of their way to help anyone. They have no sense of responsibility.

When they see someone badly injured they would not rush to help. They won't call for an ambulance and always feel justified in not doing so, usually offering an explanation along these lines: "I didn't cause the injury so I'm not responsible." They have no compassion for the suffering of other people, and they never blame themselves. They justify their *moral apathy* and do not believe that there really are people who are compassionate and willing to be helpful to others.

Passive sociopaths are not active criminals and they don't intend to cause suffering, but they have no feeling for others, and they usually believe that everyone else feels the same way. Once a patient of mine told me he forged checks and assured me that everybody would do the same if he or she knew how it could be done.

Some years ago, when I taught and supervised residents in psychiatry, I once had to suggest to a resident that he make a career change or undergo psychotherapy himself because he had no compassion for his patients. My rules were simple: Psychotherapists must not get involved with their patients' private lives, but *must get involved with the problems the patients bring to therapy.*

Passive sociopaths are not violent, but they encourage violence. They greatly contribute to the sociopathic epidemic.

Let me, at this point, quote Norman Cousins:

"We can reexamine the indifference to violence in everyday life. We can ask ourselves why we tolerate and encourage the glorification of violence in the things that amuse us and entertain us. We can ponder our fascination with brutality as exhibited hour after hour on television or on the covers of a thousand books and magazines. We can ask why our favorite gifts to children are toy murder weapons.

"We can ask whether we are creating an atmosphere congenial to the spiraling of violence until finally it reaches a point where living history is mauled and even our casualness toward it is pierced."

Some Personality Problems

Hypochondriasis

Being selfish and overconcerned with their self-being, sociopaths tend to be preoccupied with their health and appearance. Quite often they seek medical help. Whenever there is the slightest real or imaginary threat to their health, they believe that they are ill. A transient cold, mild indigestion, or any feeling of discomfort drives them to the doctor's office. Almost all sociopathic patients I have seen in over forty years of clinical practice were definitely hypochondriacs, and most of them were referred to my office by physicians who could not discover any physical ailment and told the complaining sociopaths that their illness must be psychological.

Sociopaths are oversensitive to pain and injury, notoriously *hypochondriacal*, constantly worry about their health, subscribe to popular health magazines and cheap medical encyclopedias, and eagerly attend doctor's offices.

Drug Addiction

At the present time there is an increase in marijuana use, especially in high schools and colleges. The use of marijuana by college students in 1967 was 5 percent, in 1974 it had reached almost 50 percent, and in 1982 it was well over 50 percent, and it is still going up. The hyperpermissive public attitude and decline of discipline at home and in school contributes to the spread of drug addiction.

Sexual Behavior

In sociopaths Eros is subservient to Ares, and sex is often combined with violence. Sociopaths are usually "polymorphous perverts," some of whom practice sexual relations with infants, senile women, and anyone available when they are sexually aroused. The "pleasure principle" of immediate gratification of needs is the main motive in the life of sociopaths, who do not care for anyone except themselves. Sociopaths have no affection or love for anyone, and their sexual behavior is directed to self-satisfaction with no concern for their sexual objects.

Inferiority-Superiority

As explained above, balanced individuals are instrumental in their breadwinning capacities; mutual in sex, marriage, and friendships; and vectorial in regard to children and people who need their help. A balanced individual does not have the need to gain control over others. He or she is perfectly satisfied in relating to other people on a give, give-and-take, or take basis; he or she accepts the limitations of his or her power and is satisfied with interdependent relations.

Sociopaths need the feeling of great power because they do not believe they have much power. Those who have adequate faith in themselves and sufficient faith in their friends do not need to have more power than is reasonably necessary for survival and for a reasonable amount of success in life. *But those who doubt themselves and others, and who suspect that others are their enemies, aspire to gain control over others. Insecure sociopaths* have no feelings for others. Their self-esteem is exceedingly low, and they believe they are threatened by others and have to defend themselves. A gifted sociopath can assume leadership and present himself as a poor, innocent martyr. This was Hitler's case. He spoke of innocent, poor Germany that was defeated in the First World War and was threatened by Jews, blacks, British, Frenchmen, Americans, and so on, and had to "defend itself" by mass slaughter of its alleged enemies.

The spread of paramilitary groups in the United States bears witness to the growing epidemic of sociopathy. The leaders of these groups believe that they have the right to do whatever they want, with no concern for other people.

Note

1. American Psychiatric Association, *Diagnostic and Statistical Manual of Mental Disorders*, 3d. rev. ed. (Washington, D.C., 1987).

3

Sociopathy in Childhood and Adolescence

A thirty-year-old married woman with a two-and-a-half-year-old child cried: "This kid drives me crazy! I don't know which is worse. I am on the verge of committing suicide."

Mrs. R. called my office asking for an urgent appointment. My secretary gave her an early appointment, and here she was, curled up in the armchair, speaking in an incoherent way. She was an attractive young woman, and a college graduate. She was married to a successful business executive.

"What happened, Mrs. R.?" I asked her. Mrs. R. wiped her tears and spoke quickly, her words interrupted occasionally with sobs. "My husband told me he wants to divorce me . . . all because of the child. Doctor, we had a good marriage, and now everything is over. What am I supposed to do? I am at the end of my wits."

The story was simple. Mr. and Mrs. R. had been married six years. As their financial situation improved, they purchased a house in the suburbs and bought expensive furniture. However, their two-and-a-half-year-old child showed no respect for the financial achievements of his father or for the high cost of furniture. With considerable zeal he attacked the new furniture. When Mr. R. came home after a busy day at his office, he couldn't help noticing the marks and dents on the new furniture, a vivid sign of his child's ardor and of the child's new boots.

The man accused his wife of a lack of consideration for their newly acquired property and for his hard work. Mrs. R., who majored in psychology at one of the colleges in the metropolitan area, defended her child's "right to express himself." She couldn't stop the child, "because," as she was told in one of her psychology classes, "frustration can lead to mental disorder," and she did not want to be blamed for her child's future psychopathology. Her husband, who majored in engineering in college, had no respect for Freud, Jung, Adler, or any other mental-health authority. In a moment of anger, he said: "It's either me or him!" Mrs. R., in despair, urgently sought my advice and guidance.

Perhaps Mrs. R.'s reaction was exaggerated, but many parents tend to blame themselves for whatever hardships their children might experience in the future. It is common today for children to blame parents for their true and imagined errors, and many a parent seeks foolproof advice. Decades ago, parents were told not to spare the rod and establish a strict reign in the household. Children were supposed to be seen and not heard, and parents were supposed to rule like ancient emperors.

Today most "experts" have swung the pendulum 180 degrees. Parents are supposed to be seen and not heard, and quite often unruly children are regarded as the epitome of mental health. Sometime ago, a colleague of mine, a psychiatrist, sought my advice concerning his ten-year-old boy who was judged to be abnormal simply because he was not extroverted. I saw the boy, who was interested in science and literature. His only flaw, according to others, was that he did not intend to, nor had he the chance to, become a bully. His personality makeup and his inclinations will probably determine his future as a scholar and a scientist.

Unfortunately, fad and fashion influence people's judgments and make them believe that there is but one way in life, and it is necessary to follow what the latest fashion dictates. The present-day "expert opinion" is that parents must *go down* to the level of their children instead of bringing their children up toward adulthood. Instead of helping parents to help their children grow up, some "experts" unwillingly and unwittingly infantilize the parents. The increasing wave of immaturity among adults turns into a flood of waywardness and disinhibition in their offspring. Misguided parents renounce their responsibility and abdicate their parental rights and obligations. Instead of using rational judgment, they follow the fad of letting the child do as he or she pleases, and encourage sociopathic behavior.

The Dual Role of Childhood

To be a child means to live in two distinct sociopsychological dimensions. On one hand, children have the right to be immature, and there is no reason to force a child into pre-mature adulthood. On the other hand, childhood is a *transitional period* toward adulthood, and woe to an individual who remains childish in his or her adult years. Some people confuse the dual role of childhood; some of them deny to their children the right to be childish, while others advocate perpetual infantilism. While both approaches are erroneous, the latter one prevails today.

I had a physician in psychotherapy who worked long hours and felt guilty at home. Whenever he was home, he didn't act like a loving parent, but rather like a guilt-ridden adolescent. He vied for his children's love, showered them with gifts, competed with his wife for their attention, and allowed them to act as they pleased. Small wonder that his children disrespected their father, took advantage of his dependence on them, and made him feel guilty whenever he refused to meet their irrational demands. The man didn't know how to stop the anarchy in his home and he didn't dare to exercise parental authority.

Many a parent lives vicariously through his or her child. The mother of a college girl who was under my care "controlled" her daughter's behavior in a rather peculiar way. She "loved" her daughter so much that she felt obligated to open her mail, wash her hair, decide what she bought and the dresses she "should wear," and "helped" her to do her homework. Some parents literally live the lives of their children.

Mr. Z., who was dissatisfied with his wife, developed a peculiar symbiotic relationship with his five-year-old son. He believed parents and children to be equal, and he tried to obliterate thirty years of difference by playing childish games and speaking baby talk. Some children brought up by such overanxious and overinvolved parents are unable to determine their own social role and are confused regarding their age and their sexual identity. Some parents, unhappy in their marital life, use their children as a battlefield, involving them in love-hate and acceptance-rejection moods, allowing their children to have infinite freedom in every way, including antisocial sociopathic behavior.

Early Childhood

The personality of a newborn child is a primitive, undeveloped, and impulsive region that Freud called the *id*. The id is the seat of vehement desires and seething impulses. It causes an immediate discharge of energies. The discharge that restores the inner balance is called by Freud *Lustprinzip*, that is, the principle of lust (usually translated as the "pleasure principle"). The immediate discharge of either libidinal or destructive energy brings relief, and it is experienced as pleasure. The *Lustprinzip* emphasizes the urgent need to obtain immediate gratification. The unbound, uncontrolled energies of the id lead to impulsive discharges of energies. Thus the "pleasure principle" indicates the general striving for pleasure and avoidance of pain, and it points to the urgency of obtaining such a pleasure through an immediate discharge of energy.

The id knows no values, no right or wrong, no moral standards, and no consideration for other people. It is a "cauldron of seething excitement." According to Freud, it was an "instinctual cathexes seeking discharge"—that is all that the id contains. Being unbound, fluid, and capable of quick discharge, the id's energy is easily condensed and displaced.

At the beginning of an individual's life, everything is unconscious. The id stays entirely unconscious forever; but, under the pressure of the outer world, some of the unconscious material of the id develops into preconscious material, and the ego emerges. "Under the influence of the external world which surrounds us, one portion of the id has undergone a special development. From what was originally a cortical layer, provided with organs for receiving stimuli and with apparatus for protection against excessive stimulation, a special organization has arisen which henceforward acts as an intermediary between the id and the external world. This region of our mental life has been given the name of *ego*."[1]

The ego derives its energy from the id. The instinctual demands of the id lead to investment of parts of its energy in objects. By identifying itself with the cathected objects, the ego "recommends itself to the id in the place of the object and seeks to attract the libido of the id on to itself. . . . In the course of a person's life the ego takes into itself a large number of such precipitates of former object-cathexes."[2]

The Origin of the Ego

Neonates are exposed to excitations that they cannot master. They become somehow dimly aware of them and feel uncomfortable and unhappy. Hunger, thirst, cold, noise, and other tension-producing stimuli flood the infant's mental apparatus and produce a state of anxiety. The infants wish to get rid of the disturbing stimuli, but they are unable to do so. Infants are helpless and cannot survive without being taken care of. The help must come from without; and the disturbing stimuli of hunger can disappear only with the satisfaction of hunger.

The neonates' mental apparatus, the id, resembles a body floating in water. Under the influence of environmental forces that act on the surface of the id, this surface changes and develops into a sort of protective shell called the *ego*. The surface unconscious material of the id becomes preconscious, and part of the primary mental processes are gradually transformed into secondary processes of the ego. But, Freud stressed, "the ego is not sharply separated from the id; its lower portion merges into it."

The infantile ego knows and loves only itself; it is primarily narcissistic. The infantile ego is only dimly aware of the external world. Gratification of needs must come from without, and hunger is satisfied by mother's milk. The infant is wrapped up in oneself and in one's own needs and, when the needs are gratified and tension removed, he or she falls asleep.

In his earlier works the term "ego-ideal" was synonymous with what Freud later called the *superego*. In the later works, however, the ego-ideal represented a part of the superego and its craving for perfection. Freud wrote in 1938: "[The picture of the ego] which mediates between the id and the external world, which takes over the instinctual demands of the former in order to bring them to satisfaction, which perceives things in the latter and uses them as memories, which, intent upon its self-preservation, is on guard against excessive claims from both directions, and which is governed in all its decisions by the injunctions of a modified pleasure principle—this picture actually applies to the ego only up to the end of the first period of childhood, till about the age of five."[3]

Origins of the Superego

Around the age of five, at the phallic stage, the clash between the id and the superego that represents instinctual demands versus the fear of punishment respectively, leads to the formation of the superego.

The ego grows and develops from a state of merely perceiving instincts toward one in which it actually controls them, and from yielding to instincts toward inhibiting them. In this development a large share is taken by the ego-ideal, which is partly a reaction formation against the instinctual processes of the id.

The fear of punishment and the need for affection and protection force the child to accept the parental demands and to "internalize" them, that is, to consider them as his or her own. These internalized prohibitions and self-restraints are "forerunners of the superego"; they contain the elements of the future superego, namely the fear of punishment, and tendency to conform to parental demands. As long as parental restrictions are not enforced, the child tends to disregard them. The fear of parental punishment and the need to have the parents' love leads to intrajection of their images.

The introjected parental figures are idealized and seem to be more powerful and more glorious than they may be in reality. In most cases the father's image (which usually encompasses the images of both parents) plays the greater role in the child's superego. Originally a new element added to and introjected into the ego, forming a part of the *superego*, gradually becomes a separate mental agency, often opposed to the ego. The superego is the "voice" of the parents and their moral standards as perceived by the child; it also represents parental wrath and punitive attitudes.

The ego-ideal is one of the elements of the superego that carries the child's admiration for his or her parents. The superego reflects striving toward perfection, and an effort to live up to the expectations of the parents.

The id is the sole source of instinctual energies; all the energy that the ego uses for its inhibiting and anti-instinctual functions is drawn from the id; the anti-instinctual forces of the superego are derivatives of the instinctual forces of the id.

The ego's attitude to the superego is, to a great extent, a replica of the child's attitude toward his or her parents. The ego needs love and affection, and its self-esteem depends on the approval of the superego. When the ego lives up to the expectation of the superego, the superego reacts with approval experienced as elation. When the superego disapproves of the ego, the aggressive forces stored in the superego turn against the ego, creating guilt feelings. Depression is self-directed aggression; it is the result of the ego being torn down by the superego. Manic bliss is caused by a fusion of the ego and superego.

In well-adjusted individuals, the superego plays the role of self-critic; it represents the conscience and socially approved norms and standards. *The superego represents the moral code of the individual.*

The adult superego must outgrow the initial parental prohibitions. The superego of a little child represents "not merely the personalities of the parents themselves but also racial, national, and family traditions handed on through them as well as the demands of the immediate social milieu which they represent. In the same way, an individual's superego in the course of his or her development takes over contributions from later successors and substitutes of his or her parents, such as teachers, admired figures in public life, or high social ideals."[4]

Being no longer a replica of infantile images of the parents, the superego of a mature individual becomes related to objective social and ethical standards by which the adult person abides. In well-balanced adults there is little if any conflict between the moral standards of the society carried by the superego on the one hand, and the realistic considerations of self-protection and survival as represented by the ego on the other. A child who does not have the choice to develop the superego remains a self-centered, narcissistic, and selfish sociopath.

Violent Behavior in Childhood

The inclination to hostile and violent behavior is innate, universal, and common to all living organisms. Newborn infants usually respond to frustration by outbursts of rage. Rage is an expression of hostile attitudes which can be temporary or lasting, offensive or defensive, directed toward others or toward oneself. Rage is an impulse to attack, hurt, torment, damage, insult, retaliate, or destroy, and it is the most frequent emotional background of impulsive, violent behavior. Not all children learn to control the hostile id impulses. Children who do not learn to control their hostile impulses are likely to become sociopathic.

Outbursts of anger in two- or three-year-old infants are usually directed against a definite target with the aim of causing harm and damage. Many an infant intentionally spills milk on mother's carpet, breaks a dish, or kicks a piece of furniture. Some infants physically attack, kick, or bite whoever thwarts or hurts them.

Failure to attain one's goals and to satisfy one's wishes creates the feeling of *frustration*. A quite common reaction to frustration is to attack the thwarting person or object. A child who hurts himself or herself at the edge of a table may strike the table, and a child deprived of a candy bar may strike the mother unless the parents help the child to outgrow the primitive id reactions and develop the ability to control oneself—the *ego*.

As the child grows older, he or she learns that a physical attack may lead to retaliation or punishment and thus bring more defeat and more frustration. A toddler who tries to hit or bite a grownup person may learn very soon the lesson of attacking a stronger adversary. Physical attacks may continue, but if they invite counterattacks or adult punishment, they may force the aggressive child to abandon or refrain from physical assaults. In many cases children shift from physical to symbolic expression of hostility. Making faces, sticking out the tongue, swearing, and name calling are hostile acts, but they represent some degree of self-restraint.

Children who develop fluency in verbal expression may use slander and sarcasm and employ their tongues in a more subtle manner. They may refrain from direct physical and verbal or nonverbal hostile behavior, and at humiliating and/or isolating the adversary.

Excessive parental permissiveness does not discourage aggressiveness. Mothers who usually display permissiveness when the child acts aggressively toward them have more aggressive children than mothers who do not tolerate aggressive behavior. The hyperpermissive mother is rewarding aggressive behavior, especially when the child is allowed to get away with aggressiveness. A rational nonpunitive and nonpermissive parental attitude reduces the danger of antisocial, sociopathic behavior in the offspring.

School Years

Educators, both parents and teachers, carry the current values of our society, and help those whom they educate to accept those values and live by them. Educators are responsible for the educational process for they carry the national cultural traditions. They make the decisions, and the children have to obey them. The educators decide what to teach and the children must obey their teachers. Education means discipline, and education without discipline is a futile process.

Education carries the crucial message of our national cultural achievements. A decline in the educational system can bring about both deculturation and serious regression.

School discipline is the guardian of the historical message of the present generation given to the succeeding generation. Children go to school in order to become adequately prepared for their future roles in society. Children go to school to learn, not to act as they please, and not to continue their childish ways or behavior. Schools must help children to grow up toward mature and responsible adulthood.

Children who enter schools have already failed to develop normal behavior, and the present-day lack of discipline hinders the development of self-discipline and encourages antisocial behavior. In the 1960s the majority of public school students were receiving an adequate education, however the growing unrest and declining discipline "turning up in almost open traffic in marijuana in many schools . . . Student violence is a small part of the trouble facing public schools."[5]

The situation deteriorated in the 1970s and 1980s. "While student misbehavior has been part of the folklore of the American school, it should be clear that we are not concerned with the usual type of school pranks and mischief, but rather by the escalation of school violence that is taking place both quantitatively and qualitatively since 1960. . . . Although attacks on teachers are illustrative of the violence problem in schools, it should be stressed that the vast majority of aggressive incidents are directed toward other students," experts reported.[6] According to O'Donoghue,[7] "one in five of United States high school students and almost one in three American boys now carries a gun, or a knife or another weapon, and the pattern of weapons carrying by students has become a national phenomenon applicable to schools in all regions." Obviously the so called blackboard jungle was not produced by children, but by their parents and teachers who failed to give them the necessary supervision and guidance.

Lefkowitz et al.[8] reported a study of third-grade elementary school children. The children, almost all of them eight years old, were picked at random. Ten years later a follow-up study supported the original hypothesis that antisocial violent behavior is a product of environmental influences and of learning processes. The research adduced adequate evidence that the children's violent behavior was increased whenever they watched violence on television.

In 1973 there were 13,070 gun murders in the United States compared to 85 cases in England and Wales, despite the fact that America has only a population twelve times larger than England and Wales. The violent behavior scores obtained for girls were almost the same as for boys.

The Commission on Violence and Youth of the American Psychiatric Association (APA) was empaneled in July 1991 to bring the body of knowledge generated during the last five decades to bear on the troubling national problem of violence involving youth. The following report was published in 1993:

> Although violence involving youth is hardly a new phenomenon in the United States, both the quantity and quality of this violence have undergone dramatic change within the past ten to fifteen years. Mere statistics cannot tell the story, but the following observations will suggest how much the parameters of the problem have altered.
>
> Homicide is the most common cause of death for young African American females as well as for young African American males. The probability of a young African American female dying by homicide is four times that of a non-African American female. A young African American male is eleven times more likely to die by homicide than a non-African American male.
>
> Children can buy handguns on street corners in many communities. In part because of this ready availability of firearms, guns are involved in more than 75 percent of adolescent killings.
>
> The intensity of violence involving children and youth has escalated dramatically. In testimony presented to APA, Mireille Kanda, M.D., who then was director of child protection services at Children's National Medical Center in Washington, D.C., noted that the rate of penetrating trauma caused by violence seen in her emergency

department increased 1,740 percent between 1986 and 1989.[9]

Children are becoming involved in violence at ever-younger ages. In a study of first and second graders in Washington, D.C., 45 percent said they had witnessed muggings, 31 percent said they had witnessed shootings, and 39 percent said they had seen dead bodies. A seventeen-year-old African American girl from Boston told a state task force that she had attended the funerals of sixteen friends aged fourteen to twenty-one who had died by violence.

Although young people are disproportionately represented on both sides of the knife or gun, it is important to consider their experiences as part of the larger picture of violence in America. By many measures, the United States ranks first among nations in its rates of interpersonal violence. The United States has the highest homicide rate of any Western industrialized country—a rate that is, in fact, many times higher than that of the country with the next highest rate. At current rates, more than 25,000 Americans are murdered each year, and homicide is the tenth leading cause of death in our nation.

In inner-city communities, violence often is dramatically evident in nightly shootings and in the daytime struggle of families to keep their children from becoming perpetrators or victims. The problem of youth violence is not limited to urban environments, however. Domestic violence, hate crimes, sexual violence, and violence among peers pose threats to children and teenagers in every American community. No one is immune to the pervasive violence in American society, although the probabilities of involvement are affected by race, social and economic class, age, geographical area, population density, and other factors.

According to Baron, aggressive models play an important role in the initiation of violence.[10] Eyewitness accounts by social scientists present on the scene during the initiation of violence suggest that they may. In many cases, it appears that large-scale aggression fails to develop until one or more "hotheaded" individuals commit an act of violence. The individuals present on the scene are often made "ready" to aggress by a strong prior provocation, powerful frustration, and other factors. However, an initial act of violence often seems to be required before large-scale rioting erupts.

Apparently, individuals are often affected by the actions or words of the others around them. In recent years, however, it has become increasingly clear that social influence can even be unintentional. There is a growing body of evidence which suggests that simple exposure to the actions and outcomes of others is often quite sufficient to produce large and important alterations in the feelings, behavior, or thoughts of observers.[11]

Adolescence

Adolescence is a period of life that roughly corresponds to the teenage years and encompasses puberty. Adolescence is a transition from childhood to adulthood. Such transition was rather short in primitive cultures and it was usually concluded by puberty rites that signaled the admission of the adolescent into the adult society. After the rites the young person was expected to start a family and take part in bread-winning and in other adult activities.

Contemporary adolescents do not earn a living, don't marry, are not supposed to beget and take care of children, and do not participate in civic and political activities of the adult society despite the fact that boys and girls ages thirteen to eighteen are biologically as mature or almost as mature as adults. They attain physical height and muscular strength equal to adults and they attain sexual maturity around that age. However, civilized societies deny to adolescents the rights and obligations of adulthood.

The discrepancy between biological readiness and the need for years of preparation necessary for obtaining the optimum level of sociocultural maturity creates adjustment problems for adolescents. While living with their parents and receiving economic support and psychological care many adolescents tend to rebel against parental authority. They are no longer children and they wish to be treated as adults. However, they are still children since they are totally dependent on their parents in an economic and legal sense, but they are no longer children in their physical and sexual as well as in their intellectual and social development.

Most physical changes take place in early adolescence. Around the eleventh to thirteenth year of age girls' bodies undergo dramatic changes. Their height increases rapidly, their hips become rounded, and the breasts begin to develop. In most cases the first menstruation occurs around the age of thirteen, followed by growth of pubic and axillary hair. Within one year after the first menstruation girls become capable of conceiving and thus become biologically mature females.

The physical development of boys comes somewhat later, and the dramatic physical changes usually take place at the age of thirteen to fifteen. There are rapid spurts in height; the shoulders get broader, the voice deepens, and pubic and axillary hair appears, as well as facial hair. Their sexual organs become larger, and in most cases fourteen- to fifteen-year-old boys can fertilize a woman.

Their physical development is quite often a source of concern for the adolescents. Quite often they are concerned with their appearance; their growth might seem to be too fast or too slow; their secondary sexual traits might not be enough or too much; and the entire process of growth might proceed in spurts making them too big or too small in comparison to their peers. Middle adolescence, which corresponds to the high school years, is full of social, sexual, and identity problems.

The craving for independence inevitably raises questions of *identity*, and many adolescents are concerned with their self-image. Unable to accept their own identity, they are often in a state of confusion.

Sometimes they get the right clues from their parents and teachers, but the need to be independent makes it difficult to accept adult guidance. Many adolescents and middle adolescents tend to develop strong allegiance to their peers paralleled with a somewhat irrational rebellion against their parents and the entire adult society. Unless they receive adequate guidance at home and at school, many of them regress to impulsive, unconsidered, and sometimes antisocial behavior.

A rebellion against dependence does not make anyone independent. Children are dependent, adults are interdependent. Young men and women who are gainfully employed and, eventually, marry and take care of their children, assume adult responsibilities, and become adult. They don't have to "kill" their fathers to become fathers themselves, but they finally resolve their Oedipal attachments by accepting adult roles.

Aggressive Behavior

In a study of antisocial behavior Wolfgang, Figlio, and Sellin[12] reported that of the 9,945 boys born in Philadelphia in 1945 who lived there from the age of ten to the age of eighteen, 35 percent committed 10,214 delinquent acts between the ages of ten to seventeen. They reported that 3,475 boys (35 percent of the 9,945) committed second offenses; 18 percent of them committed five or more offenses, 25 percent four offenses (or more), 35 percent committed at least three offenses, and 54 percent of them committed at least two offenses. Eighteen percent of the offenders were labeled "chronic offenders," apparently sociopathic youngsters.

Many adolescents whenever provoked, annoyed, or frustrated, act impulsively and become aggressive. There is, however, a definite difference between occasional acting-out followed by guilt feelings, and the frequent antisocial behavior of sociopathic adolescents who experience no guilt feelings whatsoever. Mosher et al.[13] in their research conducted on college students distinguished between those who believed that aggression is immoral and experienced guilt feelings, and those who had low or no guilt feelings. The individuals who had no guilt feelings could be classified as sociopaths.

Sociopathic adolescents often practice indiscriminate aggressive behavior. It is not always a reaction to frustration or elicited by anger; aggressive behavior gives them the craved feeling of power.

Parental brutality is often a highly relevant etiologic factor. Some disturbed parents excessively mistreat the child who eventually develops into a sociopathic, antisocial personality and acts out his or her rage against the persecuting parent. Some school-age children exposed to parental violence tend to direct their rage against the parents and other people. Many of them become aggressive adolescent murderers.

Aggressiveness does not start in adolescence. As mentioned above children from broken homes, those from homes full of hatred, and children who feel unwanted and insecure may act out their hostile impulses. As long as the children were little, their parents practiced coercion and corporal punishment, and the kids were forced to exercise self-restraint. But as the children became bigger and stronger than their parents, the balance of power in the hostile home environment tipped to the adolescents who acted aggressively in and out of the home.

It seems, therefore, that contemporary adolescents don't

feel very secure if there is violence in the home. Certainly members of underprivileged minority groups feel less secure than their more fortunate peers, and all statistics prove that a much-higher level of antisocial behavior exists among members of minority groups. The MacIver Report on juvenile delinquency in New York firmly rejected the notion that African Americans and Puerto Ricans were prone to violent delinquency. Moreover, MacIver found that juvenile delinquency among Puerto Ricans in New York is twenty times as high as it is in Puerto Rico.[14]

The high rate of violence is not related to any particular racial, ethnic, or religious group. The Puerto Ricans in Puerto Rico don't feel rejected or discriminated against or looked down upon. The less adolescents feel secure, the more they are inclined to display and abuse the primitive power they have—the power of their muscles. Poverty-ridden, disrespected, underprivileged adolescents may tend to bully their classmates and terrorize the neighborhood. Basically, violence serves survival and it is applied in the animal world to get food and defend oneself against being turned into food. Among human beings violence is some-times used as a cover for the fear of being weak and fear of appearing weak. Thus, a display of power and aggression "for kicks" gives sociopathic adolescents an illusion of omnipotence. "The contemporary form of violent groups reflects a brand and intensity of violence that differentiates it from earlier gang patterns. The 'kill for kicks,' homicide is today a source of concern not only in the large city but also in the suburbs and small towns."[15]

The delusion of unusual power is typical for little infants

and manic-depressive patients; in either case, the need to feel omnipotent is rooted in a profound feeling of weakness in infants, and a secondary feeling of helpless depression in adult psychotic patients. Adolescents who feel secure make good academic progress and get along well with parents and peers, and do not indulge in violent behavior.

The rate of violence among black teenagers is higher than among white teenagers, but the rate of violence is growing for all races and all social classes. According to the *New York Times*, the arrests on gun charges for children ages seven to fifteen increased by 75 percent from 1987 to 1990.[16]

The Federal Bureau of Investigation reported that the rate of violent crime between the ages of ten to seventeen increased over 25 percent in the last decade. Mr. Gransfield, a police chief in suburban Maryland, describing violent groups of middle-class teenagers, said: "The youth violence is sort of a reflection of all of society. The tolerance level seems to have gotten to an all time low."[17]

At the present time, homicide is the leading cause of death among New York City youth ages fifteen to nineteen years and the second leading cause of death among this age group nationally. During the 1980s, the rate of firearm-related homicide increased more rapidly among this age group than did any other cause of death. The 1991 national school-based Youth Risk Behavior Survey indicated that 26 percent of students in grades 9 through 12 reported carrying a weapon at least once during the thirty days preceding the survey. To more effectively target violence-prevention programs for youth in New York City, in 1992 the city's

Department of Health, its public schools, and the Centers for Disease Control conducted a survey of violence-related attitudes and behaviors among a representative sample of the city's public high school students. This report summarizes the results of the survey:

During the 1991–92 school year, 36.1 percent of all 9th–12th grade NYC public school students surveyed reported being threatened with physical harm, and 24.7 percent were involved in a physical fight anywhere (including home, school, and neighborhood). Overall, 21 percent of students reported carrying a weapon such as a gun, knife, or club anywhere 1 or more days during the 30 days preceding the survey; 16.1 percent of students reported carrying a knife or razor; and 7.0 percent reported carrying a handgun. In comparison, rates for violent and potentially dangerous behaviors were substantially lower inside the school building (being threatened, 14.4 percent; carrying a weapon, 12.5 percent; carrying a knife or razor, 10.0 percent; being involved in a physical fight, 7.7 percent; and carrying a handgun, 3.7 percent) and when going to or from school.

Compared with all 9th–12th grade students, students who were involved in a physical fight in school during the 1991–92 school year were less likely to believe that apologizing (38.1 percent versus 19.0 percent) and avoiding or walking away from someone who wants to fight (55.5 percent versus 35.5 percent) were effective ways to avoid a physical fight, and they were more likely to believe their families would want them to hit back if someone hit them first (56.9 percent versus 77.9 percent). Compared with all 9th–12th grade students, students who carried a weapon inside the school building during the 30 days preceding the survey were more likely to believe that threatening to use a weapon (21.4 percent versus 43.9 percent) and carrying a weapon (19.9 percent versus 47.9 percent) were effective ways to avoid a physical fight; were more likely to believe their families would want them to defend themselves from attack even if it meant using a weapon (43.6 percent versus 67.5 percent); and were more likely to feel safer during a physical fight if they had a knife (29.6 percent versus 64.2 percent) or a handgun (26.5 versus 60.5 percent).

Editorial Note: The findings in this report indicate that violent behaviors and weapon-carrying among youth are substantial problems in both school and community settings. The rates for physical fighting and weapon-carrying among NYC public high school students reported here are consistent with national surveys. The national health objectives for the year 2000 target reductions in homicide rates (objective 7.1), assaultive injuries (objective 7.6), physical fighting (objective 7.9), and weapon-carrying (objective 7.10), among adolescents and for increasing violence prevention education and intervention programs in schools (objective 7.16) and communities (objective 7.17) (5). In addition, National Education Goal 6 for the year 2000 is for all schools to be free of drugs and violence and to offer a disciplined environment conducive to learning.[18]

College Years

The transition from childhood into adulthood was never a very easy task, but the complexity of modern societies creates additional difficulties for the youth. The age of *physical maturation* did not change much in the course of a millennium, but the concept of *psychosocial maturity* underwent substantial changes.

Physical and sexual maturity is attained today at the age of fifteen to eighteen for boys, thirteen to sixteen for girls, but boys and girls in their teens are unable to support themselves nor are they capable of assuming responsibility for family relationships. A technological society has no use for juvenile shepherds and hunters, and the modern economic system is based on skilled labor and highly qualified managerial and professional cadres. Prolonged schooling is needed for economic adjustment and adequate psychocultural maturity is a prerequisite for adult participation in modern societies. Such social-economic-cultural maturity requires a high-level psychological development, which can hardly be attained in one's teens. Adolescent and postadolescent years are a period of frequent conflicts as young people tend to believe that they are adults and should therefore be granted the status of adults.

This process of self-assertion leads to a breaking away from parental authority. Adolescence is the first step of this rebellion; late teens and the postadolescent period is the second step. The first step is, usually, wholly negative; adolescents may try to do whatever seems to be contrary to parental wishes; they may break, intentionally, parental prohibitions and indulge in juvenile pranks while still depending on their parents economically and psychologically.

The postadolescent rebellion goes much farther and it is a more serious problem. A fifteen- or sixteen-year-old youngster may think that the older generation is obsolete, but he or she still depends on "grown-ups." At twenty or twenty-one years one may actually break away from his or her parents, become economically self-supporting, enter meaningful relations with another person, of the opposite sex, and assert independence.

Such a "rebellion" against dependence actually does not make anyone independent but *dependable*, that is, adult. Young men and women who are gainfully employed and, eventually, marry and take care of their children, are adults. *They assume adult responsibilities, thus they become adults.*

Young people at the age of eighteen to twenty-five are adult enough to critically examine social and political issues. They have attained not only physical but also intellectual adulthood, and they are capable of developing mature and lasting personal and sexual relationships. They are not adolescents any longer; the fact that they attend colleges shows that they are of superior intelligence, which may be a contributing factor in their critical attitude toward the established social order.

Superior intelligence can hardly be the sole causal factor in rebelliousness. Middle-aged people are usually more productive than destructive, and many of yesterday's revolutionaries turn into today's conservatives. One can hardly divide the world into bright revolutionaries and dull conservatives.

Age is, undoubtedly, a relevant factor in rebelliousness, and adolescence is the developmental stage at which Oedipal impulses come to the surface. In most cases this rebellion against adults comes to an end when the rebels themselves become adults. Thus, a political philosophy that puts its hopes on youth plants its trees in the quicksands of changing times. Revolutionary philosophers and ambitious and unscrupulous politicians may find young people more susceptible to their ideas and more inclined to partake in irresponsible actions, but youth as such cannot be a dependable carrier of any significant political program for the very simple reason that, fortunately, no one remains young for too long a period of time. Sociopolitical reforms are carried by more lasting pressure groups, such as, for example, nationalistic, political, and labor movements, which plan their actions carefully and seek the support of large segments of the population, irrespective of their age.

The active participation of a great many college students in protests against a variety of sociopolitical systems in Britain, the United States, France, Japan, Germany, and in Latin American countries proves that sociopolitical issues are not the crux of the matter. The world we live in is full of conflicts, and young people should be given credit for their sensitivity to what they perceive as justice.

However, they are not alone in the demand for change. All progressive people in this country and overseas, *irrespective of their age*, are keenly aware of hunger, war, and injustice and are not mere passive onlookers; *craving for social reforms is not an age-related privilege*. Young people, however, become isolated when they put forth exaggerated demands, when they take the law into their own hands, when they disrespect the rights of others, and when they use methods of terror. Disruption of classes, harassment of professors and students, "occupation" of buildings, and damage to university property and documents cannot bring any significant change in the distribution of economic wealth, in the social class system, or in the rights of minority groups. College disorders neither change the national constitution nor bring about a profound change in a nation's socioeconomic system. Rebellions, no matter what cause they advocate, are outbursts of impatience and intolerance, directed in a haphazard, often senseless manner against coincidental targets on the campus. Civil rights are not identical with uncivilized riots. The riots are sociopathic behavior.

Overstayed Adolescence: A Sociopathic Symptom

The purpose of higher education is to help gifted young people to attain the highest level of mental development and acquire skills that enable them to climb the social ladder in technological societies. Whether in America or Great Britain or India, France or China, education is today what inherited knighthood used to be in the Middle Ages. Despite distinct differences in political philosophies and social systems, ours is the era of computers, jets, and space travel, and *know how* is today what aristocratic titles used to be. Automation, Sputnik, supersonic jets, biochemistry, heart surgery, synthetic materials, and electronics are the noble emblems of our times. And those who can produce these new and necessary goods and services become the modern upper class.

Gifted students given the opportunity attain a higher

level of development, but this high level requires additional education. Those who aspire to become nuclear physicists, biochemists, physicians, electronic engineers, computer specialists, psychologists, or experts in finance, law, architecture, and neurosurgery need years and years of training well beyond their high school adolescence.

College students are young adults. Unless they are emotionally disturbed, they have left behind their adolescent immaturity, negativism, and rebelliousness. They are capable of participating as equals in any interpersonal relationship; however, due to the fact that they aspire to reach higher levels, they are compelled to continue their dependent role.

It's not surprising that many people who are otherwise adult but whose life conditions perpetuate childhood dependence, develop the overstayed adolescence syndrome. And this is the paradox of higher education: *while preparing young people to attain the highest possible level of adjustment, higher education sometimes perpetuates the conflict between two social roles, one determined by one's physical and sexual maturity and the other related to one's inability to attain full and responsible participation in adult life.* Some of the students rebel by rejecting adult styles of wear; some grow their hair long in defiance of parents and barbers; some develop a pseudosophisticated hippism; and still others invade university offices. Sociopathy is a frequent symptom.

While college students are, generally, brighter than their peers and more aware of current social, cultural, and economic issues, they exercise *less control* over their lives than their noncollege peers. A twenty- or twenty-two-year-old factory worker, postal clerk, or longshoreman can make valid decisions concerning his or her future; the future of a college student, however, depends on grades given by some university professor. Working youth can join a labor union in a struggle against the employer; student organizations have had, so far, little influence on planning and guiding the life on the campus. The institutions of higher learning are usually governed by social appointees and faculty who bestow upon the students all the benefits of science *without giving the students*, who are recipients of all the cultural goods, *the right to have even a consulting voice in matters concerning their future.* Certainly students cannot assume the role of professors, but there is hardly any rational explanation for treating them as if they had nothing to say about their future careers.

It cannot, therefore, be surprising that a great many college students resent being treated as children while they are not children any longer. Most of them cope with this problem in a rational way. Some of them, however, act in a way resembling adolescent rebellion against authority, and some get carried away and act in a destructive manner. Although the process of self-assertion is a product of normal growth, exaggerated and unrealistic plans, demands for excessive liberties, use of force, and outbursts of violence may be indicative of sociopathic personality.

History, both old and recent, offers a great many instances when abnormal individuals incited destructive wars in the name of lofty ideals. Many a gifted sociopath gave vent to his pent-up hostility under the guise of a crusade, holy war, defense of revolution, or supreme justice. Bloody wars and massacres of innocent people have been initiated by gifted but disturbed fanatics who, in the name of whatever ideals they professed, sacrificed thousands of human lives.

Torquemada, Savonarola, and Calvin in the past, Hitler, Himmler, Eichmann, Dzierzynski, Stalin, and Beria in our times professed to kill people in the name of some fanatical beliefs. Young people are usually more prone to embrace radical ideas and may therefore fall prey to unscrupulous fanatics and their demagogic methods.

The trouble lies, therefore, not in the traditional rebellions against tradition but in the disruptive nature of present-day rebellions that practice violence and terror. The self-righteous and antidemocratic character of some of the rebellions brings back much too recent memories of terror against Jews, democrats, socialists, and, later, the entire civilized world. Radical slogans do not necessarily represent justice, and forces of brutality, once unleashed, follow their own logic of destruction. The Nazi movement has had close affinity to nihilistic, hippie-style, going-back-to-nature youth (the Frei Deutsche Jugend Bewegung). Nazism is an abbreviation for National Socialism. Misguided youth may go astray, and unchecked adolescent outbursts may end in crimes against humanity.

Presently some societies prevent adolescents from becoming adults, and in so doing they perpetuate selfishness, lack of concern for others, and sociopathic behavioral patterns.

NOTES

1. Sigmund Freud, *An Outline of Psychoanalysis*, trans. James Strachey (New York: W. W. Norton & Company, 1949).

2. Ibid.

3. Freud 1938.

4. Freud 1938.

5. *U.S. News & World Report*, December 2, 1968, p. 372.

6. Harootonian and Abter 1983.

7. O'Donoghue 1995, p. 701.

8. Monroe M. Lefkowitz et al., *Growing Up to Be Violent: A Longitudinal Study of the Development of Aggression* (Elmsford, N.Y.: Pergamon Press, 1977).

9. American Psychiatric Association Commission on Violence and Youth, *Violence and Youth: Psychology's Response* (Washington, D.C., 1993).

10. R. A. Baron, *Human Aggression* (New York: Plenum, 1977).

11. Ibid.

12. M. E. Wolfgang, R. M. Figlio, and T. Sellin, *Delinquency in a Birth Cohort* (Chicago: University of Chicago Press, 1970).

13. D. L. Mosher et al., "Hostility, Guilt, Guilt Over Aggression and Self-Punishment," in *Journal of Personality Assessment* 44 (1980): 34–40.

14. Lewis Yablonsky, *The Violent Gang* (New York: Macmillan, 1962).

15. Ibid.

16. *New York Times*, March, 1992.

17. Davis 1991.

18. Centers for Disease Control Survey.

4

The Causes of the Rise of Sociopaths

Genetics

One is tempted to look for a potential role of genetic factors in antisocial behavior, and for a while some scientists assumed that antisocial delinquent behavior is inherited. Cesare Lombroso (1835–1909), professor of psychiatry and later of criminal anthropology at the University of Turin, Italy, developed a theory of genetic origin of criminal personality. He maintained that certain physical characteristics such as a flat nose, big jaw, and some other traits are typical for the "born delinquents."[1]

At the present time there is no evidence for a genetic origin of antisocial behavior, although violence can be produced by a variety of causes, and it is not limited to sociopathic people. Moreover, according to Lochlin et al., "[N]o recent study has established the inheritance of antisocial

93

personality. . . . The bulk of juvenile delinquency arises from environmental factors, but a subgroup of juvenile delinquents, who go on to become adult criminals, may have a genetic liability. . . . Longitudinal studies indicate that primary grade children with a diagnosis of attention deficit disorder are at high risk for later juvenile delinquency and a teenage diagnosis of conduct disorder, the childhood version of antisocial personality disorder."[2]

Violence is a universal pattern of living organisms. All organisms fight to eat and against being eaten. Excessive violence can be related to a variety of factors and in certain cases belligerent behavior can be related to genetic predisposition, or some organic defects. Antisocial violent behavior can be related to a low level of arousal, to epilepsy, to faulty metabolism, to brain tumors, to prefrontal lesions, to high levels of testosterone, and to other biosocial and biochemical factors. However, these are *possible* instances, *but undoubtedly the majority of antisocial cases are related to psychosocial factors.* However, not every case of antisocial behavior indicates sociopathy, and not all sociopaths are violent. Sociopaths are excessively selfish, antisocial, have no concern for others, and no feeling of guilt no matter what they do. Sociopathy indicates a lack of moral development.

Moral behavior is always related to one's attitude to one's fellow human beings. Morality starts with "I and Thou";[3] it is defined as concern and care for others. A human being can have concern for other people and their rights, or have concern only for oneself and none for others.

Mental Disorders

There are three basic types of human interaction: (1) to get, (2) to give and to get, and (3) to give.

In the first type of interaction, one's aim is to satisfy one's own needs; it is *instrumental*. In the second type, the give-and-take type of relationship, one's aim is to satisfy one's own needs as well as the needs of the other person; it is *mutual*. In the third type, the aim is to meet the needs of the other person; it is *vectorial*.

The newborn child must be taken care of; his or her needs are thoroughly instrumental. As children grow, they gradually learn to give and to get, and their behavior becomes mutual. Taking care of children is vectorial.

Well-adjusted adults act in an instrumental manner in their breadwinning activities, in a mutual manner in marriage and friendship, and in a vectorial manner in parental and idealistic activities.

One may summarize the three types as follows:

1. The first type, which is taking, the *instrumental* (I), is applicable to business associations.

2. The second, to both give and get, is labeled *mutual* (M); instances are friendship and marriage.

3. When people's objective is to satisfy the needs of others (giving without taking), it may be called *vectorial* (V); the mother's relation to the child may be considered vectorial.

Serious and lasting distortions lead to three types of mental disorder: *hyperinstrumentalism*, *dysmutualism*, and *hypervectorialism*. The hyperinstrumental type of mentally disturbed individual is a *taker*, and corresponds to sociopathy. The hypervectorial type is a *giver*, even in situations in which people usually take. These two types cover all that has been labeled schizophrenia and related conditions. The third type, the dysmutual, is highly inconsistent, since they tend to overdo in *giving* while at other times they overdo in *taking*; this type of disorder is what has been called the manic-depressive.

The sociopathic disorder is the *hyperinstrumental mental disorder*. It is basically a severe regression to infantilism where one is exceedingly selfish and is unable to develop mutual and vectorial attitudes.

My studies of families of sociopathic patients (hyperinstrumentals) reveal a peculiar lack of warmth and a lack of contact between the parent and the child; who became a sociopath. Such a child grew up in an essentially isolated environment. From his earliest years he was forced to take care of himself, never to experience the security that comes from having human friendship, sympathy, and affection.

Sociopaths have never had a stable social relationship in childhood. Their life histories, whether they were reared in splendor or in squalor, resemble the lives of wayward children. They have developed no attachment to anyone because there were no trustworthy, stable, and friendly figures with whom to identify.

In several cases the mother was severely disturbed and unable to care properly for the child; in many instances the sociopathic child exploited and ridiculed the sick mother. Hyperinstrumentals are never proud of their parents; tender feelings toward them are virtually nonexistent.

Hyperinstrumentals believe that they are innocent, hungry, lonely, and mistreated creatures. Given to cowardice, they fear confrontations with equals but do not hesitate to attack those who appear defenseless. Whether or not a hyperinstrumental will become a criminal depends largely on circumstances. He or she is a *criminal at heart* who will or will not commit a crime depending on the weakness of the victim and the danger involved in the attack. Most hyperinstrumentals avoid antisocial acts for which they may be punished: when they are caught, they regret not the crime but the punishment.

The outstanding trait of hyperinstrumentals is their extreme narcissism. The dysmutual manic-depressive, having failed in the attempt to give love, tries to get love by alternating love and hate toward oneself and others. The hyperinstrumentals are concerned neither with giving nor receiving love. They want food, whether it is given with or without love; they want sex, with or without affection; and what they want most are material possessions, comforts, and power.

Hyperinstrumentals treat people as if they were tools to be used or food to be eaten. They could never be friendly toward weak people; friendliness on the part of the strong ones makes them suspicious. Sociopathic patients may not trust the friendly attitude of their own therapists. One patient suspected that the psychotherapist was better disposed toward wealthy patients, and another therapist who acted in a friendly manner toward all his patients was believed to be stupid. Hyperinstrumentals do not believe that anyone can be genuinely friendly, honest, or self-sacrificing. They are convinced that the world is a jungle full of shrewd, selfish, and greedy beasts. In such a world everyone must look out for himself or herself, selfishness and greed being condoned as necessary self-defense strategies.

The hyperinstrumentals use violence not only for tangible gains. Their deeply rooted feelings of inferiority, combined with lack of love, motivates them to hurt others not only for money or other gains, but also for a show of power. Hyperinstrumentals may kill their victims even after robbing them. They often torture and mutilate in robbery and rape because cruelty enhances their feeling of power. When their perception of reality declines, they turn psychotic and attack, torture, and murder, displaying inhuman cruelty and deriving great pleasure.

Sociopaths do not experience any feelings of guilt. They know neither regret nor self-accusation on moral grounds, though they may hate themselves for being weak or for not being shrewd enough to escape punishment. Feelings of depression in hyperinstrumentals can originate in a loss of property, failure in business or school, loss of a job, fear, feelings of weakness and inadequacy in the face of danger, inability to cope with a job, failure to escape penalty, and so on. Lacking in remorse or repentance, sociopathic depression does not resemble the self-torturing accusations of the hypervectorial or dysmutual. Hyperinstrumentals, convinced of their innocence, rarely, if ever, feel that they deserve punishment.

The hyperinstrumental personality structure precludes normal development of a higher level of sexuality. Thus most hyperinstrumentals remain fixated on infantile sexual levels. For the most part, their inner conflicts originate in fear of others. Having no moral standards, they are guided by a desire to avoid disapproval; this fear is the only inhibitory factor that prevents sociopaths from acting out their impulses. The pleasure principle, that is, the principle of immediate gratification of needs, is the main motive in the life of sociopaths.

A forty-year-old male patient practiced sex with animals, children, men, women, with whoever and whatever sex objects were available. He knew society condemned his behavior, but he himself did not feel that he was wrong. His only fear was that of being caught; therefore he neither raped nor killed. He did maintain, however, that if he could get away with murder, "he certainly would commit it." A sociopathic woman, married, twenty-eight years old, was having, as she put it, "occasional" affairs with men. She was not interested in anyone, and she was essentially frigid, but when men were "nice" to her, flattered her, bought her little gifts or just impressed her, she saw no reason for being faithful. "As long as my husband did not know," she said, "he was not hurt."

When the hypervectorial mind is flooded by the primary unconscious process, the resulting confusion is largely confined to the emotional or affectual spheres. Even a disturbed schizophrenic may retain some degree of objective thinking and continue his or her studies or occupation. In hyperinstrumentals, unconscious processes do affect their understanding of the outer world and intellectual functioning; they regress to childlike behavior.

An inadequate development of the superego in

sociopaths is related to the lack of opportunity for identifying oneself with parental figures. One of my patients was brought up in an institution that preached religious devotion while practicing the law of the jungle. The officers and counselors of this children's home ate very well while the children often went hungry. When doing their kitchen chores, the children could compare their own meager food with the luxurious meals of their educators. The shortage of food and lack of educational guidance led to a general practice of thievery; whenever children did not appear on time at their table, their food was stolen by other children.

The children wore shabby clothes all year round, with the exception of days when important visitors were expected; then clean bedspreads, neat tablecloths, and special "visitors" clothes were distributed.

A sociopathic child may identify with a strong aggressor. A young patient identified with the "smart tough guys" who knew how to take advantage of other people, but could not identify with his middle-class parents who were unable to provide any guidance. This patient tried to abstain from violence because of its dangerous implications, but he would not refrain from cheating, theft, drinking, and sexual abuse.

Another patient, a middle-aged man, grew up in a peculiarly disorganized family in the Midwest. Both father and mother had "boyfriends" and "girlfriends"; they were divorced, remarried, and again divorced. They did not part, but lived together in a common-law marriage with several children, practicing overt promiscuity. The patient was actively engaged in homosexual relations and occasional heterosexual relations with juniors. Another man forged checks but he would deceive only the wealthy ones. He refused to steal from poor men because "it was not right." His moral standard reflected the norms of his parents' neighborhood where stealing was taboo.

Sociopaths who belong to a social group with a clear-cut moral code are less likely to hurt others because this would jeopardize their social status and be detrimental to their interests. Thus many sociopaths lead the lives of honest citizens not out of integrity but because it is "more advantageous" to stay honest. However, should an opportunity for getting away with a crime arise, they are quick to seize upon it. Sociopaths abstain from dishonesty, unfairness, and violence for one reason only: the fear of retaliation. They practice all kinds of dishonest deals; they are the bookies, loan sharks, dope peddlers, swindlers, and extortionists. Some of them combine crime with respectable and legitimate business. While they fear being caught and punished, they are incapable of experiencing guilt.

What prevents moral development? What favors antisocial, sociopathic personality? What encourages antisocial behavior?

We have already noted that antisocial behavior does not always require a genetic predisposition; the inclination for belligerent behavior is universal. And all living organisms act offensively to eat and defensively in order to not be eaten. One can safely assume that every newborn human being carries the tendency for violent behavior.

Further on, each of us requires certain definite developmental phases combined with life experiences to mobilize the defensive-offensive inclinations and become a well-adjusted person who can relate to others in an instrumental, mutual, and vectorial manner. It is a long process.

Obviously, sociopathy is a lack of, or a reversal of, the developmental process and a regression to a primitive, not-yet-human hyperinstrumental behavior. Sociopaths can be bright, gifted people who have achieved a high level of development in many areas, but remain at or regress to primitive levels, and to an antisocial way of life. *They are hyperinstrumental.*

There is no connection between one's IQ and moral behavior. Some criminals are very bright, but they act in an excessively selfish manner, with no consideration for the rights of other people.

According to the American Psychological Association Commission on Violence and Youth, the *breakdown of family processes and relationships* contributes to antisocial behavior, including violence.

> *It is difficult to separate the respective roles of inherited factors, acquired biological factors (such as birth trauma or head injury), and learned psychosocial factors in the development of violence....* Whatever the balance between the contributions of nature and nurture, it is likely that a model stressing the interaction of these factors will most accurately describe the development and continuity of aggressive and violent behavior patterns.... Family characteristics and a breakdown of family processes and relationships contribute to a foundation for the development of antisocial behavior including violence.[4]

The Role of the Family

My studies of sociopaths point to a lack of parental affection in childhood. When Robert came home telling his mother that a kid beat him up, the father didn't want to listen to "a jerk," and the mother punished him for not fighting back. The father would brag about "fooling" his customers, and whenever his wife, the boy's mother, disagreed with him, he hit her.

When Robert reached the age of twenty-three and had his own income, his friends convinced him that he needed psychotherapy. After a few therapy sessions he told me that his father insisted on seeing me. His father intended to "help me" by giving a detailed description of the boy's life experiences. When the father came to my office, he described in detail his own "brilliant mind, heart of gold, and financial success." He tried to convince me that he was a "great man" married to a mentally retarded woman, and that no one recognized his divine virtues. He never said a word about his son.

Morality means caring and helping; no society could survive if its members didn't help each other. The newborn infant is totally selfish, totally narcissistic, in urgent need of care, and unable to reciprocate. As infants grow, they usually learn to go beyond their primitive selfishness. They *begin* to love their parents and the others who take care of them. They usually develop the ability to interact with parents, siblings, and playmates. Rational parental care helps the child's normal development.

Moral behavior protects human lives. The growth of

sociopathic behavior is a threat to the survival of our society. Human behavior is motivated by the *lust for life* and the two driving forces: Eros (love) and Ares (hate). Well-adjusted people care for themselves and for others. They are balanced in their selfish-unselfish behavior and are willing to protect themselves and others.

Moral behavior implies concern for other people. The need to survive, the *lust for life* is the main motivating force in human life. Moral behavior, the care for others, is not a luxurious whim; it is a *necessity*, a prerequisite for human survival. No human being can live alone, and all human beings need cooperation with other people. Democratic society allows virtually the same degree of freedom for all its members, and advocates moral concern for one another. Moral behavior is a necessity in the family, in the up-bringing of children, and in all types of human interaction.

Even the best seed will not develop in arid soil. Seeds need fertile soil, and children need care and guidance. Parental care and a positive attitude help the child to feel secure and develop gratitude and affection.

A decline in *family bonds* and in *parental authority* pre-vents development of the child's normal behavior. Inade-quate parenting is the *chief cause of the decline of moral behavior and the spread of sociopathy*. Family life is the chief factor in the child's personality development. In 1995 the rate of divorce reached 60 percent, and the rate of out-of-wedlock childbirths is reaching 30 percent. These are distinct psychosocial factors that indicate a serious decline in family life and its potential role in promoting normal, responsible, moral behavior.

The Current Crisis

Today's rise in sociopathy is related to the decline of the modern family which fails to give the children adequate guidance. In the past, children were expected to stay at home while they were dependent, stay at home a little longer while they were earning their first wages, and then move, not too far away, into their own homes to do a job very much like their father's in a familiar social setting. In the past there was a gradual transition toward independence, through working and wage-earning, which was the first assertion of responsibility.

Today we often make our children economically dependent long after the age of childhood and adolescence. Our complex society demands a long period of initiation. Thus the process of initiation becomes a long exclusion from initiative. We deny the young real responsibility, and try to compensate them by giving them "free time" in which they can "do what they like."

Sociopaths did not have affectionate human relationships in childhood. No one has ever cared for them throughout their younger years and no one has ever loved them. They could not develop affection and attachment to anyone because there was no one affectionate to them and no one who encouraged an affectionate relationship. In many instances the mother was severely disturbed and unable to care for the child. In many other cases the mother left the child with relatives, nurses, or just alone or on the street. Adult sociopaths are neither proud of their parents nor do they have tender feelings toward them. This applies to children of slums and of wealthy suburban families alike; the lack of parent-child close bonds makes the children grow up without having experienced feelings of belonging and gratitude. Sociopaths do not care for their aging parents. They do not feel that they owe anything to sick and old parents. They do not feel affection for anyone; they probably have heard the word "affection," but they have never experienced affection, haven't loved anyone, and didn't believe that anyone loved them.

Wealthy Families

Some sociopaths come from families rich in money and poor in love who did not teach the child moral values or foster inhibitions of impulses. The sociopaths learn to get whatever they want without consideration for others. Vacillating, morally weak, hyperpermissive, and uncaring parents foster selfish, sociopathic personality development. A description of a young sociopathic patient may elucidate the point.

The nineteen-year-old man who took LSD sat in my office, and admitted taking hallucinatory drugs. He was in a state of panic; he felt he was losing his mind.

"Doc," he whispered, "what else could I do? What is this all about?"

He trembled. He was both scared and bewildered. He came to me asking for help, wanting to get rid of the unbearable tension and the terrorizing fight.

He was a bright young man, a student at a private university. His father was a real-estate broker, his mother was a socialite, and his older sister was married to a business executive. They lived in a mansion in a fashionable community on Long Island. They owned three new cars and belonged to a country club. The father was a board member of a charity organization and the mother was president of a church sorority.

Prolonged emotional deprivation and parental rejection are crucial factors in the development of the narcissistic-instrumental type sociopath. Parental rejection fosters extreme narcissism. Thus "it is the narcissism, resulting from rejection, which accounts for the inability of the child to form an object relation to his mother in the first year of life, to his siblings later, and to others."

Most psychoanalytic studies indicate the lack of maternal love as the main determinant in the development of a self-centered, narcissistic personality. Children who did not receive maternal love tend to withdraw interest from objects and remain fixated in a primitive personality structure. Failing to develop a superego, they remain unable to experience guilt feelings for antisocial behavior.

According to Karpman, "[P]sychopathic development for the most part indicated a clear-cut psychogenic relationship with inadequate opportunity in the first years for the establishment of a meaningful primary mother relationship of cathexis . . . the absence of accepting parents who . . . provide the child with the capacity or wish to become socialized."[5]

A weak or defective superego is regarded by Eissler to

be the product of parental misguidance or the lack of guidance.[6] A mother's self-contradictory, unpredictable, and
shifting emotional attitudes, or frequent substitutions of
maternal figures, all interfere with healthy identification
and formation of an adequate superego. The presence of an
inadequate superego explains why children appear to experience very little anxiety. Superego deficit, together with
extreme hypercathexis of the self, are not conducive to
internalization of fear, which is the basis of anxiety. Should
a hyperinstrumental person ever feel guilty, his guilt feeling
is immediately projected and the blame is placed on the
allegedly hostile environment.

Levy distinguished between the "deprived" and
"indulged" psychopath.[7] The emotionally deprived child is
unable to identify with his or her parents or parental substitutes. He or she develops a weak superego and is unable to
exercise moral self-control. The child who is allowed to do
as he or she pleases and grows up without any restraint is
similarly unable to control impulses and is likely to become
aggressive and antisocial. The identification with his or her
indulging mother is responsible for the overpermissive
superego that does not act as an inhibitory factor.

Quite often sociopaths who were brought up in an
atmosphere of interparental fights feel rejected by parents
who resented the burden of taking care of their offspring.
Some underprivileged families create an atmosphere where
the jungle ethic prevails and the entire world seems to be
populated by enemies. However, children of well-to-do
families where the parents have substituted money for
affection and nurturance may become sociopaths. They

grow up in a home where no one loves them and they have no one to identify with.

There are two family settings which breed sociopaths: either in substandard slum dwellings or broken homes where the child had no one to obey and no one to identify with, or with wealthy parents who bribe their children but do not guide them. In the first case, the child grows up in a "sink-or-swim" atmosphere; in the second, the child develops no self-restraints and no consideration for anyone.

Parental Rejection

Some parents do not want the children that they have. The children are often rejected and treated with abuse and neglect, which contributes to the child's feeling of insecurity and undermines the child's self-confidence. Some children feel that parental rejection is justified. The rejected child may feel weak and helpless. He or she distrusts others because there is no reason to trust or like anyone. A prolonged and severe rejection produces in the child feelings of mistrust that can lead to sociopathic justification of hostile behavior. In order to protect oneself and overcome the feeling of inadequacy, the sociopathic child may resort to aggression. If he or she is strong enough and by aggressive means can assert him(her)self and receive a feeling of power, they will continue the aggressive behavior. Rejection from one's parents may convince children that humans are hostile and aggressive, thus justifying the children's antisocial behavior in their own eyes.

Undoubtedly inadequate parent-child relationships contribute to sociopathic personality. The sociopathic child fails to accept social controls because of parental ineffectiveness at socialization of their child. When the child's parents typify the community to the child, he or she is likely to become an aggressive, rebellious, hostile, and hyperactive person and engage in delinquent activities.[8]

Parental attention and affection are signs of love and interest. When a child is not able to obtain attention at home, the child may resort to aggression. There is a direct relationship between inadequate attention in the home and aggressive behavior. Children brought up in homes where little attention is given to them tend to display a higher level of aggression.

Maternal Deprivation

Every child needs an affectionate relationship with the mother. If a warm relationship is not established, anxiety feelings result in a state of "maternal deprivation." Severe deprivation results in anxiety and in strong feelings of anger and hostility.

Maternal rejection and emotional instability frequently appear in the case histories of delinquents. Wilson's study of "problem families" in Cardiff, Wales, has revealed maternal deprivation in every home that produced a juvenile delinquent.[9] When the mother is absent, neglectful, ambivalent, or insecure, the child fails to receive some stable "source of satisfaction." The child withdraws his or her love from the object-world and places emphasis upon receiving narcissistic pleasure. The future sociopath tends toward "rocking, sucking, and masturbation."

When the mother ignores the child's emotional needs, the child does not trust her. If the child fails to receive love and affection, the oral-sadistic impulses become directed toward the mother, and sociopathic children often develop hate for their mothers. When they perceive her as one who rejects and hates, the hatred toward the mother may be expanded to include the external world.

The child's ambivalent image of the mother as one who does not care increases the child's hostile feelings. Many a sociopath uses projection as a defense against the self-consuming rage and despair, and the hatred usually extends to include the entire world. The lack of love, replaced by intense hatred, prevents the sociopathic child from developing a superego-conscience necessary for adequate social interactions.

The hostile attitude toward one's parents fosters sociopathy. The child fails to identify with the parent and thereby fails to internalize the parents' values and a superego. Behavior which might displease the parent is not inhibited, but may instead yield gratification and pleasure, and the parental image is no longer an acceptable model for conformity.

Parent Against Parent

Does exposure to violent parental behavior elicit similar actions on the part of the child? This issue has stimulated two distinct, yet closely related lines of research. The first has sought to determine whether exposure to live, aggressive models plays an important role in the occurrence and spread of collective violence, while the second has investigated the impact of massmedia portrayals of violence—especially those on television—upon the behavior of viewers. Evidence relating to both issues is abundant.

Children who witness parental aggressive behavior learn that antisocial behavior is the right behavior. My sociopathic patients report that witnessing their parents' verbal and physical violence helped them become convinced that this was their usual way of life. Their parents never expressed guilt feelings. Apparently guilt feelings are hollow, nonexistent experiences of past times. Dishonesty, lying, and cheating were the usual actions of their parents' daily life, combined with occasional physical violence. Quite often the parents encouraged their children to be dishonest as long as the dishonesty was successful. One young woman reported that her parents told her to form a gang, steal other children's money in school, and physically hurt her adversaries. A male sociopathic patient who witnessed his father's frequent physical assaults told me that his mother criticized the adolescent boy. "What kind of a man are you?" she yelled. "Why don't you take a knife?"

Spousal Abuse

According to Goldstein and Krasner, "While research on the incidents and factors associated with marital violence has grown in the past ten years, the development of a comprehensive theory which explains the acquisition and maintenance of marital violence has received relatively less attention. . . . Because traditional theories of spouse abuse focused on the 'masochistic' needs of female victims and 'psychopathic/sadistic' personalities of their male assailants, numerous family and societal factors are neglected."[10] "Most of these men are low in self esteem, they may be particularly so in situations which threaten their male authority."[11]

Violence between parents is highly conducive to violent behavior in children. When children witness their fathers beating their mothers, they tend to develop the belief that one has the right to use violence in order to attain one's objectives. Usually physical interparental violence is accompanied by verbal accusations, and the attacking fathers maintain that they had a reason to beat their wives.

According to Krauss and Krauss, "[R]esearch into the prevention of violence has recently become an American national priority . . . and the Centers for Disease Control and Prevention recently joined mental health and social service systems to *prevent* interpersonal violence. . . . In 1984, 10.7 percent of children had been victims of a severe violent act," and in 1993 "34 percent of adults witnessed a man beating his wife or girlfriend." "Some adult sufferers witnessed or were victims of violence as children."[12]

In the United States, 102,555 cases of rape were reported to police in 1990. About 14 percent of American women were raped, and at the present time every five to six minutes a case of rape is reported to police. More cases of sexual assault and rape are perpetrated by boyfriends or husbands. "The social and economic costs of the physical effects of male violence against women . . . in the United States suggests that they can be staggering. . . . [W]ife battering is the single most common case of injuries to women requiring medical intervention in their childbearing years."[13] The apparent increase in domestic violence greatly contributes to the rise of sociopathy.

According to a 1993 national poll, 34 percent of adults in the United States reported that in their childhood years they had witnessed men beating their wives or girlfriends. About 30 percent of women reported physical abuse. According to Russo, Koss, and Goldman, "We estimate one in four wives is physically battered. It is also estimated that some form of violence will occur at least once in over half of all marriages, with 3 to 4 million American women battered each year by their partners."[14]

Child Abuse

The arrival of a child who demands care is often perceived by one or both parents as an intrusion on their "rights." Attention combined with shifting attitudes of attraction and repulsion are showered on the child. In many cases, men look for outside sources of affection and direct all their hatred to their wives. Women who have children bestow on their offspring a great part of their frustrated rage. Children are sensitive to nonverbal communication and somehow are aware that the mother wishes to get rid of them and be free again. Many married couples stay together "for their children's sake" and use their offspring as a convenient battleground.

A rejected child may end up with a nervous breakdown, but most children are made of more sturdy stuff. Many a rejected child develops the mentality of a hunted animal. It is sink or swim; "either I get them or they will get me." Extreme selfishness, cunning devices, lying, and exploiting other peoples' weaknesses become the only way the child believes he or she can survive. This sociopathic mentality which is so frequent in our society and practiced under the slogan "if you can get away with murder, why not?" is usually a result of extreme parental rejection. I saw sociopathic individuals coming from broken homes in low socioeconomic classes. On the other hand, in wealthy families where the father and mother live side by side with each other, each of them wrapped up in making and spending money, they offer very little affection to their children. Children who grow up in a world of emotional neglect and alienation may turn to a wayward life, with or without drugs, indiscriminate sexuality, and desperate futility. The parents of sociopathic children are not necessarily sociopaths, but the intraparental alienation or animosity often leads to a total neglect or rejection of the children.

Some parents use their children as defenseless targets. A thirty-five-year-old patient reported that whenever his father had business difficulties, his mother was the father's target. Usually it started with the father complaining over dinner that the soup was cold, or he blamed his wife and attacked her verbally and sometimes physically. Afterward he punished his wife, had a drink, and went to sleep.

Then the mother turned to the ten-year-old boy: "Why didn't you defend me? Are you a man or a lamb? Why didn't you fight this son-of-a-bitch?" When the boy tried to defend himself, the mother hit him and shouted, "I don't have to feed a traitor!"

At the present time, close to 500,000 children in the United States need protection against being abused.

Children physically mistreated by their parents learn to use violence to coerce others to obey them. Being forced to obey, they learn that violent behavior can help them to attain their goals. The fact that their own parents, who are expected to be kind and loving, practice hurtful violence leads to the formation of a self-righteous behavior. The parents who hurt them justify their behavior and maintain that their actions are not hostile but conducted in the name of love. They tell the beaten child that beating will make him or her into a "better human being." The parents justify their cruelty, thus convincing the child that one is allowed to act in an otherwise reprehensible manner provided one has a sort of excuse.

The process of identification with the aggressive parent leads to the formation of a hostile, self-righteous superego (a diminished conscience). Beaten children learn that they have the right to do as they please in order to attain whatever goals they may have. The idea that the "end justifies the means" becomes the guiding motive in their self-righteous and antisocial sociopathic behavior.

According to Prothrow-Smith, "the destructive lessons parents teach when they are physically and psychologically abusive to their children and when they allow their children to be physically and psychologically abusive to others with our society's glorification of violence . . . set our children up to be the perpetrators and the victims of violence."[15]

According to the American Psychological Association Commission on Violence and Youth,

> [P]arental rejection of the child, and inconsistent and physically abusive parental discipline all seem to contribute to early aggressive behaviors. Lack of parental supervision is one of the strongest predictors of the development of conduct problems and delinquency. Parents who support the use of aversive and aggressive behaviors by children and fail to teach nonviolent and effective methods of solving social problems contribute to the development of coercive family interactions and to later patterns of antisocial behavior in the child.
>
> Harsh and continual physical punishment by parents has been implicated in the development of aggressive behavior patterns. Physical punishment may produce obedience in the short term, but continued over time it tends to increase the probability of aggressive and violent behavior during childhood and adulthood, both inside and outside the family. These findings suggest a cycle in the development of aggressive behavior patterns. Abuse at the hands of parents leads children to think and solve problems in ways that later lead to their developing aggressive behavior patterns and to their continuing the cycle of violence.[16]

Mr. T. was an executive who could find time for everything and everybody except his wife and their fourteen-year-old son. Mr. T. came to my office seeking help in his sexual and domestic problems. He complained of loss of authority and respect in his home. His wife had taken over the reins; she did not heed his advice and rejected his sexual advances. The fourteen-year-old son showed total disrespect for his parents, stayed out at night, took drugs, and used obscene language.

One day, Mr. T.'s son and his friends attempted to steal a car and were caught by police. Mr. T. asked me to see the boy. The boy came to my office, accompanied by his mother. They engaged, in my presence, in a dialogue in which the mother pleaded with the boy to give up the "bad company" that "pulled him into mischief." The boy told his mother "to mind her business"; he would not allow parents to mix in *his private life*. When the mother pleaded, "You embarrass your father," the boy burst out laughing and yelled, "How about you? Don't you think people don't see how you treat Daddy?"

When Mrs. T. asked the boy to behave, the boy replied with a barrage of curses: Mrs. T. wept. The boy looked at his mother and then turned to me. He said, "Dr. Wolman, do you see what kind of parents I have? They mix in my private life and tell me what to do! My mother wants me to be home every night at 10 o'clock! Tell me, what would you do if you were my father?"

"I would not allow you to speak to me the way you spoke to your mother," I said.

"I wouldn't care for a father like you," he said.

"Do you care for your father?" I asked.

"My father? He doesn't say anything! He is my mother's slave!" the boy shouted. "I can do anything with my father! Why wouldn't you let me do what I want?"

Some fathers believe that their parental responsibilities end with signing checks and paying bills.

Mr. F. was a kind man who did not realize that, whereas his day was full of challenges, achievements, and frustrations, his wife's day was full of often exasperating frustrations. He struggled all day long with numbers, cash flow, and complex figures.

One day when Mr. F. came home his mind was preoccupied with complex business affairs. He did not notice that his wife had put on a new dress and was trying to get his attention. When his seventeen-year-old daughter announced at the dining table that she won a prize for an English composition, he replied with an absentminded smile. His ten-year-old son was rebuffed when he asked his father to take him to a ball game on Saturday, for Mr. F. had much business planned for that day. His wife became irritable and his daughter had tears in her eyes. His son mumbled curse words under his breath. They ate in silence.

After dinner, he sat for a while with his wife, trying to listen to her. He was tired; and his wife's wave of demands—concerning the stove that needed repair, the gardener who failed to show up, and the gifts for his parents' anniversary—put him to sleep.

"You are never home," his wife's shrill voice woke him up. "And when you come home, you are not with us. You're just a boarder here!"

"I am doing it all for you, for our children," Mr. F. begged. "Please understand. In a couple of years we will be really okay. Just give me a chance."

"I just don't care anymore," Mrs. F. replied. "I'd rather be poor and have a husband than be rich and alone as I am now."

When their seventeen-year-old daughter was brought by Mrs. F. to my office, that particular evening was described by the girl in detail.

"My mother always worries, always complains. Am I responsible for her misery? She says she doesn't have a husband. What can I do? I am worse off. I have no one. I have neither a mother nor a father.

"After the dinner, when Mother left the living room in a huff and my father was very upset, I tried to cheer him up. I wanted to show him my school essay in English. I got an A+ and a special reward. Guess what happened. My father took the paper, glanced at it, and said, 'Very good.' Do you think he read it? That would be too much for him. But he reads *Forbes*, *Barron's*, and God knows what! The only thing he cannot read is his own child's essay."

The Teenage "Culture"

Lack of guidance and parental overpermissiveness forces adolescents to seek support and stability somewhere else. Many of them come to senior high schools and colleges with little faith in and no respect for adults. The contest of wills at home usually ends with the victory of the "younger generation." Small wonder that some of them try the same "method" with regard to teachers, professors, school administrators, public officials, and society at large. Those who feed and clothe them and put money in their pockets are called "the establishment."

Receiving little if any moral guidance, being brought up without restraint, and having received inadequate encouragement for self-restraint, some contemporary American adolescents perpetuate the pattern of selfishness and instrumentalism. Unable or unwilling to transmit whatever cultural and moral values they possess, many contemporary parents passively watch the erosion of the cultural heritage of the Judeo-Christian tradition and continue paying their "children's" bills in silent resignation or subdued anger.

However, in many instances the so-called teenage culture is a product of the affluent society that has created a huge leisure class of youngsters. The teenage culture is a leisure-class culture in which the social role of the students is representative of prolonged adolescence.

One of the main values and status symbols of this leisure class is the possession of a car. It is almost a prerequisite for popularity, a necessity for dating, and a sign of distinction in the adolescent crowd.

Some contemporary teenagers are interested in sports, automobiles, clothing, dating, popular music, sex, and drugs. Drug abuse has become a favorite enjoyment at any age, and some parents punish their child for stealing drugs from parental cupboards. Lack of purpose, sexual license, and economic parasitism are essential ingredients of the sociopathic youth "culture." Youth groups with their own activities, practices, and standards often look to their peers for approval and support, and to the mass media (controlled by adults) for solutions to their problems. The high schools

and the colleges are often gathering places for teenage interests and activities. The traditional task of education—preparation for the responsibilities of adult life—has lost its
prime importance.

Posters depicting animal copulation, "Make Love—Not
War," are widely distributed in America, imitating in a
peculiar way the "mature" practices of "adult" stag parties,
wife swapping, encounters, marathons, sensitivity, and
plain orgiastic practices closely resembling Fellini's
Satyricon.

One can't help wondering, do early sexual relations
indicate early maturity or do they delay or prevent an
overall maturation of personality? Early and unrestrained
sexual practices are common among baboons, rhesus mon-
keys, and other infrahuman species, and some primitive
tribes. It seems, therefore, rather strange to accept the sociopathic regression to primitivism as a sign of allegedly progressive and revolutionary ideas.

At puberty and in early adolescence, sexuality cannot be
based on a lasting and rational choice of a partner, and it
cannot attain for an adult integration of physical desires
with appreciation of another person. It takes years of intellectual and emotional development before the adolescent
reaches sociopsychological maturity and becomes capable
of developing a close and lasting bond with another person.
Early sexual relations resemble picking a not-yet-ripe fruit
instead of waiting for it to become ripe. Sociopathic adolescents have very little if any self-control.

In the one-parent family, the family must reorganize its
domestic and economic responsibilities, and its system of

affectional and emotional support. In one-parent families the mother (who is more often than not the parent) is also the provider. Mothers must work to support the family and in a great many cases the children live in an empty home with no one to relate to.

In 1960 approximately 5 percent of American children lived in single-parent homes with their mothers. In 1970 the figure more than doubled to 12 percent of American families having one parent, the mother. In 1993 the figure more than doubled again: 26 percent of American families are mother-only households. The situation is worse in black families: in 1970 the mother was the only parent in 33 percent of black families. In 1993 mothers headed 58 percent of black single-parent families. Single motherhood is on the rise, giving the children less economic support, less attention, less protection, and less guidance.

Time magazine describes the situation as follows: At the present time "more children will go to sleep tonight in a fatherless home than ever in the nation's history. Talk to the experts in crime, drug abuse, depression, school failure, and they can point to some study somewhere blaming those problems on the disappearance of fathers from the American family. . . . The Census Bureau can document the 70 million mothers age 15 or older in the U.S.A., but has scant idea how many fathers there are. . . . It's a nonexistent category. It's the ignored half of the family."[17]

Sociocultural Issues

Sociopathy did not start today. Chapter 5 will describe sociopathic behavior in past times, but at present we are facing a dangerous rise in sociopaths.

The current spread of sociopathy calls for a detailed analysis of what causes the epidemic. Obviously a conflict of present dimensions can't be related to a single factor, but *inadequate parenthood* is undoubtedly the main factor. The decline of family life in the United States has reached unheard of dimensions; *today 70 percent of marriages end in divorce, and 30 percent of children are born out of wedlock* according to *Time* magazine:

> Crime has become Public Enemy No. 1, a bigger concern to most people than joblessness or the federal deficit. All over the U.S. citizens are buying alarm systems, installing window bars and escorting their offspring from school to soccer to Scouts. In a *Time*/CNN poll, 89 percent of those surveyed think crime is getting worse, and 55 percent worry about becoming victims themselves. . . .
>
> In recent months, violence-ridden cities from New York to Los Angeles have enjoyed sizable decreases in crime in general and murder rates in particular. Part of the explanation is that federal agencies like the FBI and Drug Enforcement Administration have shrunk their headquarters' staff to attach more agents to local police. FBI Director Louis Freeh credits "safe streets" campaigns in 117 communities for reducing crime rates by breaking up street gangs. . . . The effect of three decades of rising crime rates has been cumulative: rare is the family that has not been scarred. "We've been living at what is a very

high plateau of criminality for a long time," says John Stein, deputy director of the National Organization for Victim Assistance. "And the American public is worn out by it." For all Americans, the odds of becoming a victim are far greater than they were in 1963, when the FBI crime index counted 2,180 reported crimes per 100,000 people. Three decades later, police agencies reported investigating more than double that number: 5,483 crimes per 100,000 people.

The most chilling sign of things to come is the rising rate of youth violence. According to the FBI, juvenile arrests for violent crime rose 68 percent from 1984 through 1993. "Never in our history have we seen this phenomenon of youth violence as random and as inexplicable," says Attorney General Janet Reno. Her prescription: more secure facilities for violent youthful offenders and follow-up after they are released. "We're going to have to support them and assist them and assist them in getting a job," she says. "Otherwise it's going to be a revolving door."[18]

Television

According to the American Psychological Association Commission on Violence and Youth: There is absolutely no doubt that higher levels of *viewing violence on television* are correlated with increased acceptance of aggressive attitudes and increased aggressive behavior. Three major national studies—the Surgeon General's Commission report (1972), the National Institute of Mental Health Ten-Year Follow-up (1982), and the report of the American Psychological Association's Committee on Media in Society (1992)—reviewed hundreds of studies to arrive at the irrefutable conclusion that viewing violence on TV increases violence. In addition, prolonged viewing of media violence can lead to emotional desensitization toward violence.

Children's exposure to violence in the mass media, particularly at young ages, can have harmful lifelong consequences. Aggressive habits learned early in life are the foundation for later behavior. Aggressive children who have trouble in school and in relating to peers tend to watch more television; the violence they see there, in turn, reinforces their tendency toward aggression, compounding their academic and social failure. These effects are both short-term and long-lasting. A longitudinal study of boys found a significant relation between exposure to television violence at eight years of age and antisocial acts—including serious, violent criminal offenses and spouse abuse—twenty-two years later.[19]

Violence on television teaches that one can get away with murder. By the age of eighteen, American youngsters have spent 11,000 hours in schools, but they have watched 18,000 TV murders! Seeing on TV how easy it is to attack innocent people encourages some youngsters to follow the path of crime.

Deculturation

Human progress has encompassed all areas of the universe with the spectacular exclusion of the human race. Having lost the not-too-well established cultural norms, contemporary man turns to escape devices. Big parties and small parties, wife swapping and mixed dorms, making money and throwing money away are no longer the privilege of the jet set, for everybody wants to be counted among the "beautiful people." Mass media paved the road for the victorious march of mediocrity and conformity.

Human relations today are regulated by statistics, television, and computers, relieving individuals from responsibility for their actions. Children are expected to comply with statistical and developmental rules imposed by some irresponsible writers whose latest device has overnight become a best-selling piece of fad and fashion. Some "scientists" have decided that children are not supposed to be children any longer and are not expected to listen to their parents; many schools are turning into blackboard jungles. Individual conscience and inhibition are dismissed as antiquated values not belonging to our modern era of disinhibition.

Physical violence and sexual license, so widely practiced in the last days of the Roman Empire, are being taken out from the catacombs and distributed by mass media, and glorified as the latest and newest pattern of natural and spontaneous behavior. Today's mass media give free-of-charge publicity to violence and celebrations. To be "in" is tantamount to aping the id-type life patterns of the "beautiful people," and acting out one's desires for sex, drugs, money, and power.

Uninhibited sex practices, greediness, and violence permeate contemporary life in a strange coexistence with spectacular achievements in science and technology. We build pyramids taller than those of ancient Egypt and create Towers of Babel that reach higher than the sky.

Violence

In the overwhelming multitude of protests and rebellious programs carried out by blacks and whites, liberals and radicals, students and statesmen, one voice comes through and merges into a single outcry: *it is the almost universal demand for change.*

What currently exists is apparently dissatisfying and frustrating, and millions of people want and expect change. A change that brings improvement is called *progress*, but not every change has been a change for the better. Consider fascism and Nazism. Consider the widespread use of narcotics and the increase of crime and violence in America. Approximately 400 people are murdered in the United States every week. In 1970 the rate of reported violent crimes was 360 per 100,000 population; in 1989, it escalated to 550.

Since no human being and no nation is strong enough to fight off all present, future, and potential enemies, piles of defensive-aggressive, traditional, and modern weapons grow. If progress is to be measured by the number of people one can kill, humanity has made fantastic strides. In World War I about 10 million were killed; in World War II over 50 million.

Endowed with superb memories, human beings carry old grudges; being brilliant, they invent murderous weapons; having an excellent system of communication, they teach their children to fear and to hate.

The more scared people become, the louder they praise war "heroes." Strong and brave men build; but weaklings and cowards find an easier way, for destruction requires little effort, endurance, and courage. Terrorist groups do not aim at reforming social systems; their acts are self-righteous temper tantrums. Quite often insecure parents who fear growing old try to prevent the growth of their children, and prefer to see them "making revolutions" rather than becoming responsible adults.

Notes

1. Cesare Lombroso, *Crime, Its Causes and Remedies* (Boston: Little, Brown, 1911).

2. J. C. Lochlin et al., "Human Behavior Genetics," in *Annual Review of Psychology* 39 (1988): 101–33.

3. Martin Buber, *I and Thou* (New York: Scribners, 1958).

4. American Psychiatric Association Commission on Violence and Youth, *Violence and Youth: Psychology's Response* (Washington, D.C., 1993).

5. B. Karpman, ed., *Symposia on Child and Juvenile Delinquency* (Washington, D.C.: Psychotherapy Monographs, 1959), pp. 143–44.

6. K. Eissler, *Searchlights on Delinquency* (New York: International Universities Press, 1949).

7. D. M. Levy, "The Deprived and Indulged Forms of Psychopathic Personality," in *American Journal of Orthopsychiatry* 21 (1950): 250–54.

8. R. A. Baron, *Human Aggression* (New York: Plenum, 1977).

9. H. Wilson, "Juvenile Delinquency in Problem Families in Cardiff," in *British Journal of Delinquency* 9 (1958): 102.

10. A. Goldstein and L. Krasner, eds., *Prevention and Control of Aggression* (New York: Pergamon Press, 1983), p. 41.

11. Ibid.

12. Krauss and Krauss 1995, p. 130.

13. National Victims Center, *Rape in America: A Report to the Nation* (Washington, D.C., 1993).

14. Russo, Koss, and Goldman 1995, p. 124.

15. Deborah Prothrow-Smith, *Deadly Consequences* (New York: HarperCollins, 1991), p. 145.

16. American Psychiatric Association Commission on Violence and Youth, *Violence and Youth: Psychology's Response* (Washington, D.C., 1993), p. 19.

17. *Time* 1993.

18. "No Parents Home," *Time*, January 30, 1995.

19. American Psychiatric Association, *Violence and Youth*, p. 33.

5

Historical and International Data

As described above, at the present time we are witnessing the rise of sociopathy and the growing danger of an epidemic. However, excessive selfishness and lack of consideration for fellow men and women are not new phenomena, and they are not limited to our country.

What we are facing are not the origins of sociopathic behavior, but their rise and the danger that they may jeopardize the future of human culture and, possibly, the future of the human race.

When the anthropologist Claude Lévi-Strauss was asked what he thought of contemporary humanity, he compared human beings to maggots in a sack of flour. With the increase of the maggot population, maggots became somehow aware of the presence of other maggots before they have any tactile contact, and begin to secrete toxins which kill at a distance. The maggots poison the flour that they inhabit, and eventually all die. Something similar, Lévi-Strauss said, is now happening to humanity.[1]

Our Culture

Culture is the way in which a society lives. The culture of primitive humans was one in which hunters and fishermen lived in caves. Our culture is technological. We build massive structures, operate factories and global information systems, and drive around in automobiles and jet across the planet in airplanes. Culture is the way a society acts in order to survive. The concept of culture includes the ways the group acts to secure food, clothing, and shelter. The ways a nation, a clan, or a tribe relate to one another in their struggle for survival are intrinsic elements of their culture.

The individual desire for survival and to remain alive with or without others is embedded in human nature and repeatedly reconditioned and reinforced. Human belligerence, whether offensive or defensive, is one of the outstanding psychological elements of the human personality.

One may hypothesize that the origin of human society was *bellum omnia contra omnes* ("the war of all against all"), but the origin of human civilization was certainly related to some sort of a social agreement (a type of social contract). Human beings have been born with the ability (or have had to learn) to live with one another, for this was *the only way that human beings could survive.*

While human beings had cooperated with one another to a greater extent than most other species, they also had more intraspecific fights than any other species. Intraspecific strife and killings are typical for only a few species, such as rats and certain kinds of fish, but they are frequent for human beings. Human history, as described in the mythology of Israelites and Romans, started with fratricidal acts; Cain killed Abel, and Romulus killed Remus. However, the way most human groups interacted was not fratricidal but cooperative. Quite early in history human groups established laws forbidding fratricidal wars and murder. The early codes of Hammurabi included punishment for murder, and the Ten Commandments stated, with utmost clarity, "Thou shalt not kill." The ancient laws of Greeks and Romans insisted on peace and forbade fratricidal murder. Even in intercity strifes, they imposed restraint and periods of compulsory peace. However, these restraints were not always successful. Selfish, antisocial, and violent behavior is not a new phenomenon.[2]

The Illusion of Power

The fight for survival is the general motivation for human behavior. The chances for survival mainly depend on the ability to obtain food and shelter, and to fight off one's enemies. Power can be defined as the ability to satisfy one's own needs and the needs of others.

Elation and depression originate in true or exaggerated feelings of strength and weakness. People are elated when they feel powerful, and they are depressed when they feel weak and powerless. Elation carries the message of power, while depression is the psychological corollary of feeling weak and angry at oneself for being weak.[3]

Violent behavior can give people an illusion of power

they do not have. Several people toil to construct a building, but one half-wit can set it afire. It takes years of tender love and care to bring up a child, but one terrorist can kill many children. It takes plenty of power to create, but it does not take much power to destroy. Small wonder that many young people and adults are easy prey for fanatics and gang leaders. Mussolini's fascist "arditi," Hitler's S.S. and S.A. gangs, Stalin's and Jagoda's henchmen, and other terrorists felt great when they killed innocent people.

There is a magnetic attraction to terrorist gangs. Joining a dictatorial cult or a terrorist gang suspends an individual's responsibility, obliterates guilt feelings, and removes moral inhibitions.

Usually human cruelty increases when an aggressive sociopath gains an uncanny, almost hypnotic control over large numbers of people. History is full of chieftains, prophets, saviors, gurus, dictators, and other sociopathic megalomaniacs who managed to obtain support from people and enslaved them. Many a historical "hero" strove for his own immortality and for the mortality of other people. Pursuing their allegedly sublime goals, many historical "heroes" fostered hostile feelings and incited people to violence. Some of them believed in their "historical mission" and thought of themselves as saviors. Sociopathic fanatics, obsessed with delusions of grandeur, motivated by a persecution complex and driven by an insatiable desire for power, led millions of people to mass murder and self destruction. The story of several "great" leaders is perhaps the most weird part of the bizarre history of humanity. Anxiety-ridden sociopathic individuals such as Tiberius,

Torquemada, Stalin, and Hitler exercised more power than rational leaders.[4]

Some students of social psychology[5] maintain that underprivileged minority groups tend to be more belligerent than others. However, members of the Ku Klux Klan do not belong to an underprivileged minority group, nor do the members of the various militia organizations. Most members of the German Baader-Meinhof gang and of the Italian Red Brigades were middle- and upper-class young people. The parental income of the American S.D.S., Weathermen, and so on was higher than the average income of parents whose sons and daughters studied at expensive colleges, and the Arab terrorists are well paid and well armed.

Many sociopaths practice violence "for kicks," that is, for self-aggrandizement. Violent behavior gives the perpetrators the feeling of power, and sociopaths don't take chances; they attack only those who cannot defend themselves. Weak adversaries provide the sociopaths with a secure and quick victory. The terrorists who murdered the single American serviceman on a TWA flight after tying him up, and the terrorists who murdered an invalid in a wheelchair on a cruise ship, were sociopaths who enjoyed an easy victory over helpless victims.

Sociopaths never attack a strong adversary. They tend to join a gang rather than act alone. Many anti-Semitic, anti-black, and other gangs who persecute minority groups are comprised of sociopaths. Not all Germans were Nazis or pro-Nazis, but the Nazis who murdered helpless civilians were selfish, hostile, and cruel sociopaths.

According to Charny, "genocide in the generic sense is

the mass killing of substantial numbers of human beings, when not in the course of military action against the military forces of an avowed enemy, under conditions of the essential defenselessness of the victims."[6]

There are several types of genocide, e.g., when the government of Sri Lanka rounded up about five thousand Tamil villagers and executed them, or when the Chinese government did the same with people in Tiananmen Square, or the Armenian genocide, the holocaust of the Gypsies, or the Nazi holocaust of the Jewish people, or the mass murder of Kurds in Iraq, or the Khmer Rouge in Cambodia, or the Soviet gulags, and so on.

Justification of Violence

Not all aggressive people are sociopathic, but sociopaths always justify their aggression and blame their victims.

When Hitler embarked on his conquest of Europe, he justified his aggression by blaming others for restraining Germany's freedom. He demanded freedom of movement, the freedom to occupy the Sudetenland, and the freedom to occupy Austria and Czechoslovakia. He maintained that Europe was a German *Lebensraum* and he was indignant at the British and French efforts to limit his freedom.

Stalin murdered his true and imaginary adversaries because their being alive could limit his "freedom of action." Emperor Nero and King Henry VIII murdered innocent people in alleged defense of their personal freedom.

Tyrants and dictators take away the freedom of others in the name of their own freedom. All oppressors and persecutors insist on their right to do as they please at the expense of others.

In the 1930s Germany was "overpopulated" and needed more *Lebensraum*. After the Second World War the Germans from Silesia and Sudeten immigrated to Germany, and there is no overpopulation at all. In the Thirty Years' War the Emperor of the Holy Roman Empire wanted to confiscate the secularized Church property, and the pious Protestant Lords joined Martin Luther in order to grab the property that belonged to the Church. The Holy Crusades, started by the inspiring words, "C'est le Dieu qui veut" ("God wills it"), were helped by the merchants from Venice and by the Byzantine rulers who paid well for the "holy" enterprise.

In the past, one had to use a sword to kill an "enemy." The Crusaders killed a couple of hundred thousand Jews. In our times, 6 million Jews and 4 million other people were gassed, and 20 million were murdered elsewhere. In the "primitive" and "barbaric" past, prior to the great advent of modern technology, world wars were unthinkable. But in our contemporary and highly civilized era we have had two world wars in one century.

Violence is not necessarily and not always associated with hatred. Julius Caesar did not hate the Gauls; he simply subjugated them. Napoleon did not hate the Spaniards; he merely wanted his family to rule the world. The Gauls hated Julius Caesar and fought against him, and the Spaniards hated Napoleon and offered a desperate resistance to his armies. Apparently the defenders hate the aggressors; do the aggressors hate their victims?

Great criminals and conquerors tend to make excuses for their aggressions. Hitler never professed hatred for Austria and Czechoslovakia; he just "needed" to occupy them. When he attacked Poland on September 1, 1939, he ordered some of his henchmen to shoot at his own border guards. At sunrise he announced on the radio that the Poles had opened fire on German soldiers "und es wird Zurückgeschossen" ("the fire has been returned"). The apparent lie had a purpose: to prevent or at least to slow down the the Allied help to Poland.

According to their propaganda, the Nazis hated all Jews, but they certainly "loved" Jewish money, the gold extracted from Jewish teeth, soap cakes made of Jewish bones, and lampshades made of Jewish skin. It is quite possible that the Nazis hated the Japanese more than the Jews, but the Japanese were powerful and the Jews had always been an easy scapegoat. The French might dislike the British and vice-versa, but the chances of a war across the channel could be substantially increased if one of the two nations would become an easy target. The Communist rulers of Russia hated Red China more than they hated Alexander Dubĉek's Czechoslovakia, but in 1968 they occupied Prague and not Beijing. The Czechoslovakians raised their fists in helpless hatred and shouted: "You are Nazis! Go home!" But the Soviet tanks imposed their iron rule over a country they did not hate at all.

Quite often outbursts of human violence resemble animal "mobbing." At the sight of an intruder, birds attack the common enemy en masse, no matter who it is. The fights between Moslems and Hindus in India, Protestants and Catholics in Belfast, and the persecution of Kurds in Iraq and Armenians in Turkey are recent contemporary phenomena.

Terrorism

Terrorism is a grave sociopolitical and psychosocial problem. Its origins are related to the dictatorial terrorist systems of Hitler and Stalin.

By following a fanatic leader the followers acquire a meaning in their lives, and thus are helped to overcome the existential nihilism of our times. The dictators and gang leaders follow the feeling of superiority (Raskolnikov's elitism) and enable their followers to look down on the rest of humanity in the belief that they have the right to act in a reckless way while serving an allegedly sublime goal. Moreover, acting in a group and following an inspiring leader reduces or even obliterates the normal feeling of guilt and enables people to practice sociopathic violence.

The lack of determination on the part of the potential victims has always encouraged the aggressors. The way Lenin and later Hitler conquered their countries should have served as a lesson, but humanity has rarely if ever learned from past errors. John Reed's book *Ten Days that Shook the World*, describes the Bolsheviks' reckless attacks on the shaky democratic system of Kerensky. William Shirer's *Rise and Fall of the Third Reich* pointed to the forceful and ruthless savagery of the Nazis and the inept and helpless German democracy.

In both cases the *appalling permissiveness* of the liberal governments encouraged the future dictators and enabled them to destroy the democratic system. *Weakness invites aggression*, but in both cases it was not real weakness. Kerensky had enough power to defend the budding Russian democracy, and the German liberals of the Weimar Republic could have fought Nazism instead of allowing the Nazis to arm themselves and impose their rule on Germany.

Helpless liberals discouraged and alienated many of their followers, whereas the determined and aggressive tyrants gained plenty of public support. *Weak people lose their friends; strong people attract them. Whoever allows people to get away with murder, invites murder.*

Continuous Violence

In America every week about 400 people are murdered. Two-thirds of them are killed in family and neighborhood quarrels or in drug and gang wars. One-third of all murders are perpetrated by strangers. The rate of violent crimes, including murder, aggravated assault, robbery, and rape, in 1970 was 360 per 100,000 population; in 1980 it was 550. Not all cases of violence are reflected in statistics, and many cases of intrafamiliar violence are not reported to police.

Violence is not the monopoly of fighting couples, neighbors, and muggers. At a high school football game in Florida an assistant school principal was shot and killed by a rival school business manager, and many sport events are concluded by fistfights and mob fights between the competing groups of fans.

The data deal with the civilized and democratic American population. In Idi Amin's Uganda, every so often an entire village or an entire tribe was slaughtered. In Khomeini's Iran, every day another individual or another group of people was executed. In the former Yugoslavia, people who lived together peacefully for years resorted to killing one other. In Lebanon, in addition to the PLO, eighteen terrorist factions murder each other. According to the CIA, there are today at least 140 terrorist organizations around the world.

In the years 1820 to 1914, wars and persecutions killed 18 million people. In World War I about 10 million were killed. In World War II well over 50 million died. *Human history is a history of a slow progress in many fields except in weapons and techniques of mass murder*, and the annual number of people killed increases. The projections for a future nuclear war are even more spectacular, for hardly any human beings will survive a nuclear holocaust.

Practically all revolutions in the past were lost as soon as they were won. Too often the price for freedom was the blood of innocent people, and the coup de grâce of Napoleon restored the rule of one man over France. Congolese people had the right to be independent; did they have the right to murder? Foreign capitalists came back to the Congo, but no one could revive the nuns and priests murdered in the Congo's revolution against Belgian rule. In the Soviet Union property belonged to the government, and perhaps there was more social mobility than there was in the old days; but the country was ruled by a small, self-appointed group of individuals whose despotic methods sadly resembled those of the old regime. People who dared to disagree with the Soviet government were sent to the same Siberia, following in the footsteps of writers who opposed the czarist governments.

One cannot correct one social ill by creating another. The theory and practice of a "revolutionary minority" that imposes its will on the masses in the name of some remote ideal of justice creates more severe injustices and abuses than the imperfect old systems. The Inquisition tortured people "in the name of"—so did Hitler, Khomeini, and other fanatics and usurpers. Disinhibited social reformers act out their "free" impulses at the expense of other people.

The present-day social climate fosters sociopathic personality distortions and encourages antisocial behavior. The two extremes, the very wealthy and the very poor, have managed to occupy the main streets of our cities and impose their valueless ways of life. The upper classes and the so-called fast trackers practice their selfish ways of life, and the government stands behind them ready to bail out a corrupt bank or a corporation with taxpayer's money. Many poor people don't look for productive life, and the welfare system has turned many of them into passive receivers of public handouts. These two extremes seem to contribute to antisocial, parasitic, criminal behavior.

Ancient Rome was a community of working farmers and artisans. The decadent Rome of later years was divided between the opulent owners of palatial properties (*Pallatium*) and the poor slum dwellers of the *Insulae*. Roman emperors bowed to the wealthy and fed the slum dwellers with handouts of bread and entertainment—"panem et circenses" ("bread and circuses"). It is not coincidental that the very wealthy parents who give their children nothing except money, and the very poor parents who neglect or abandon their children, foster sociopathic behavior in their offspring.

Contemporary civilized and democratic societies have developed an ultrapermissive attitude that, in a way, condones and even encourages license and violence. It seems that by a gross misinterpretation of liberalism, some modern societies foster disinhibition and regression.

Quo Vadis, Humanitas?

Where does all this violence lead us? Do we need another war? Do we need a war of all against all, a *bellum omnium contra omnes*? What happened to social rules of behavior? Must the selfish, self-righteous, belligerent sociopaths win and put an end to human values and to humanity? What can we do?

Notes

1. Claude Lévi-Strauss, *Structural Anthropology* (New York: Doubleday, 1967).
2. Francis A. Beer, *Peace Against War: The Ecology of International Violence* (San Francisco: W. H. Freeman, 1981).

3. Benjamin B. Wolman and G. Stricker, eds., *Depressive Disorders* (New York: John Wiley & Sons, 1990).

4. Benjamin B. Wolman, *Call No Man Normal* (New York: International Universities Press, 1973).

5. Kurt Lewin et al., *A Dynamic Theory of Personality* (New York: McGraw-Hill, 1933).

6. I. W. Charney, "Toward a Generic Definition of Genocide," in *Conceptual and Historical Dimensions of Genocide*, ed. G. Andeopoulos (Philadelphia: University of Pennsylvania Press, 1984).

6

What We Can Do: Public Responsibility

The Growing Danger

The rise of sociopathy represents a serious threat to civilization and to the democratic way of life. It seems that our indecisive, hyperliberal, and hyperpermissive attitudes encourage the spread of sociopathic behavior and jeopardize our way of life.

According to Dilulio, the actual number of rapes, robberies, assaults, burglaries, and other crimes suffered by Americans in 1993 was 43,622,006. From 1985 through 1993 the murder rate increased by 65 percent among eighteen- to twenty-four-year-olds and soared a terrifying 165 percent among fourteen- to seventeen-year-olds.[1]

In 1992 over 6.6 million violent crimes were committed, but just 3.3 million were reported to police, and only 165,000 perpetrators were convicted.

Some people believe that permissiveness, forgiveness, and love can stop antisocial behavior, and kindness should inspire people to do whatever they can for the kind people. Obviously, no one can be kind and loving forever and for everyone, and not all people are grateful to kind people. The religious slogans of "love thy neighbor" and "love thy enemies" carry a sublime and wonderful message, but they have not been very successful so far. The question is *how* to prevent self-righteous and hostile behavior.

Even the United Nations, the hoped-for international guardian of peace, is not very successful in assuring peace and preventing violence. Little wars and major wars go on unabated in the Middle East, Africa, Latin America, eastern Europe, Northern Ireland, and inside many countries. Despite agreed upon and highly publicized international rules, Iraq and other countries are still armed with chemical, biological, and probably nuclear weapons.

Limited Morality

Some people show concern for members of their family. Some people are willing to take care of members of their clan or clique. Some people believe that they are obliged to protect members of their religious denomination, and ethnic and racial group. Some people believe that it is ethical to persecute Jews, blacks, and others, and advocate "white superiority." The numerous paramilitary organizations in the United States and the cults in America, Japan, and everywhere else, view their hostile and violent acts as morally justified. And what is going on today in Bosnia and Kosovo proves that one does not need to be a Nazi to practice genocide. One must state that moral behavior is *either universal or nonexistent*. The *goal of ethics is the survival of all human beings* and the limitations are self-contradictory, a betrayal of fundamental moral rules.

Consider prejudice, bias, and xenophobia. If a party, or a nation or some group A practices moral behavior *within* the group and denies it to group B, group B must do the same. The members of group A may believe that killing members of group B is not immoral, and the same reasoning applies to group B. So who is moral? Who is right? In Bosnia every one of the fighting groups maintains that it *has the right to have its way*.

Similar analyses should be applied to any type of self-righteous group. According to Dostoevsky's hero, Raskolnikov, average people should abide by the law, but "extraordinary individuals" have the right to disobey any law and can do whatever they believe is right to do. The question that should be asked is, who is the extraordinary person? The elitist philosophy has inspired every warrior who believed in his or her *exclusive* right. How about competing warriors? Who was right: Antoninus or Augustus? Napoleon or Nelson? Unfortunately, this type of rationalization goes on, and many a religious sect, a national group, or a political party can continue their elitist views, teaching sociopathic behavior to the younger generation.

Moral behavior is either universal and unlimited, or it does not make any sense at all. The rule "Thou shalt not kill" assigns the *right to life to every individual*. As long as any human society is unfair, intolerant, and prejudiced; as long as there is discrimination against Jews, Kurds, blacks, or anyone else, such a society is immoral and encourages immoral, antisocial, sociopathic behavior.

Every single exception breaks up the entire system and brings us back to the mentality of the caveman. It is not true that in Nazi Germany everybody murdered everybody. It is also not true in regard to any organized gangsterism, such as the Mafia, or piracy. Criminal gangs have their codes, but they are criminal because they practice extortion, violence, robbery, and murder in regard to *some people*.

Thus one can't help being shocked whenever well-meaning civil rights groups, acting on what they believe to be their right, request freedom of speech for neo-Nazis, or other individuals who incite crime and violence. Freedom of speech is a freedom for peaceful disagreement, but not a freedom to incite to murder.

What Hitler asked for was his *freedom* to use German military power to murder Jews, Czechoslovaks, and other people, to plunder Poland, to subjugate Europe, and to enslave the world. Unfortunately, well-wishing people let him go far ahead in his plans.

The Meaning of Freedom

It is necessary to repeat that when Hitler started his wars against the Poles, the French, and the British, he wanted freedom for himself and slavery for others. He struggled for his *own Lebensraum*, assuming that there was not enough room for the Germans in Germany. The Germans had to spread around the world like lemmings and destroy everything in their path.

Today, despite this imaginary overpopulation, Germany is a blossoming country and has a most prosperous economy, while in Hitler's time, with a much smaller population, Nazis were hungry for new conquests and new territory.

Democracy is based on an equal restraint on the freedom of *all* individuals. Were each individual free to do what he or she wished, the social group would plunge into continuous war of all against all. Since the human species is particularly belligerent, and its levels of self-control and inhibitions are not particularly high, a society that permitted complete freedom for all its members would end in mass murder, which is tantamount to mass suicide. All societies must practice some degree of restraint because such restraint is necessary for their survival.

Even primitive societies practice cooperation in hunting and fishing, in agriculture and industry, in peace and in war. All societies impose some sort of coexistence rules between their members by erecting a system of justice and by policing. All societies impose laws and all legal systems represent a certain minimum morality in consideration for one's fellow human beings.

Legal systems can be more or less democratic, and more or less concerned with the well-being of all; but no society can tolerate complete chaos and freedom for all.

The wishy-washy liberal attitude is an invitation to violence. Our ultrapermissive attitude is perceived as a sign of weakness, and *weakness invites aggression*. Our democratic country still allows the formation of *private armies* that ultimately might destroy democracy. Some people believe that this is the way to practice democracy, while they practice self-destruction. Democracy does not mean unlimited freedom to organize self-righteous sociopathic gangs; *democracy means the same freedom for all, while dictators and terrorists practice all freedom for some.*

The proliferation of drug abuse and violence are dangerous signs of regression to infrahuman modes of behavior. The contemporary proliferation of gangs whose members take the law into their own hands and destroy a public building may indicate that *homo sapiens* is an endangered species. However, the problem is as much with the impostors, fanatics, and self-styled leaders as it is with their *followers*, for hardly any gang leader could have become a menace to humanity without followers.

The Attraction of Power

As explained before, violent behavior gives people an illusion of power they do not have. Hundreds of people toil to erect a building, but one half-wit can set it afire or bomb it. It takes years of tender love and care to bring up one child, but one terrorist can kill many children in a matter of seconds. It takes *real power* to create, but it does not take much power to destroy. Small wonder that many young and immature people can easily become prey for fanatics and gang leaders.

There is, however, another and even more magnetic attraction in terrorist gangs. Following a fanatic leader removes the individual's responsibility. Joining a cult or a paramilitary gang suspends individual conscience, obliterates guilt feelings, removes moral inhibitions, and fosters sociopathic personality type. These people tend to assault, bomb, and kill, and it is easy to incite them to a pogrom of Jews, a lynching of blacks, the beating of gays, the burning of churches, and the like.

What Can We Do?

World War II came to an end in 1945. In 1947 Bertrand Russell wrote: "We have been taught to take Evil seriously. It is neither our fault nor our merit if we lived in a time when torture was a daily fact. Chateaubriand, Oradour, the Rue des Saussaies, Dachau, and Auschwitz have all demonstrated to us that Evil is not an appearance, that knowing its cause does not dispel it . . . that it can in no way be diverted, brought back, reduced, and incorporated into idealistic humanism."[2]

Preventive Action

One may indulge in lofty dreams of peace on earth, but preaching cannot produce significant change. Prevention is the only rational approach that can bring a substantial reduction in antisocial acts.

The *basic preventive method is based on exterior*

restraint. Not the after-the-fact punishment, but a strong and determinate protective system can deter potential muggers, rapists, and murderers. A forceful and efficient protective force can secure peace, freedom, and safety for millions who are not criminal. The wars against Hitler and Saddam Hussein were the moral obligation of humanity, for morality must be defended. Moreover, in order to stop antisocial behavior *long-range preventive action is needed. This action* must start at home and be supported by schools, enabling the children to develop *heteronomous* morality. Mass media; youth centers; religious, cultural, and political organizations must embark on a far-reaching program of moral education.

Where Are We Now?

The era of territorial conquests, colonial empires, and military splendor is over. Wars have become too expensive to wage and victories are too futile to aspire to. The great upheavals of the past have become obsolete and the biggest protest marches cannot feed even one hungry mouth. The cemeteries are full of Napoleons, Caesars, and Alexanders who believed they were indispensable, but history does not bow her head any longer to generals.

The world does not need naive dreamers, prophets, and world saviors. The facts are clear; wherever there is life, the fight for survival goes on. Animals kill other animals to eat, and animals fight against being killed for food. Nature knows of no morals, no manners, no consideration; the big ones eat the smaller ones, the smaller eat the smallest, and all living organisms fight for survival. *But human beings can get whatever they need without fighting*: they can *produce* whatever they need, and the democratic way of life can offer equal opportunities for all people.

The self-styled idea of elitism and of being extraordinary human beings must be counteracted by a universal repudiation and condemnation of terror and terrorists. Terrorists crave publicity, recognition, and glamour; they are actors on a big stage, and they applaud themselves and expect public applause. A universal disrespect, disgust, and condemnation will frustrate their hopes, and a united, determined, and forceful attitude will make them realize the futility of the game they play.

We need not passively wait for destruction of our democratic way of life. Democracy was not born overnight. Humanity struggled for centuries along a tortuous road toward the democratic system of law and justice. Weakness invites aggression, and we must not repeat the errors of the past. We are for freedom of speech, but not for freedom of action. We are willing to listen to everyone's *words*, but we shall not allow anyone to be killed by *swords*.

Two hundred years ago Edmund Burke said: "The only thing necessary for the triumph of evil is for good men to do nothing." The International Organization for the Study of Group Tensions is calling on all men and women of good will to join us in the search for solutions—to prevent and to stop the growing wave of violence. We do not promise an easy victory, but we are here, ready to do our job. We shall never surrender.

How to Restrain Violence

Violence must be restrained. The rule "Thou shalt not kill" applies to everyone, thus "No one shall kill you." The alternative is that everyone might be killed. The rule "Thou shalt not kill" is the prerequisite for survival, and every society— from the most primitive to the most civilized—must regulate interpersonal behavior.

One can distinguish several levels in the way societies have restrained violent behavior. The earliest and the most widespread method has been the use of force that prevented and/or punished for the use of violence. *Fear* has always been and still is the main and fundamental restraining factor; fear of being frustrated by overwhelming force restrains violence. Sociopaths do not attack powerful adversaries, but weak and helpless individuals—the easy targets.

A society that practices indulgence encourages crime and fosters violence. A society where people "can get away with murder" fosters sociopathic behavior. Inadequate protection of human lives and property invites violent behavior, and a flimsy, inconsistent, overpermissive, and procrastinating judicial system creates a social climate conducive to sociopathic, antisocial acts.

In 1835, J. C. Prichard published *A Treatise on Insanity and Other Disorders Affecting the Mind.* Prichard introduced the term *moral insanity*, defined as "madness consisting in a morbid perversion of the natural feelings, affections, inclinations, temper, habits, moral distributions and natural impulses, without any remarkable disorder or defect in the intellect or knowing and reasoning faculties and particularly without any insane illusion or hallucination."[3] At that time perversion of "natural feelings" implied antisocial behavior. In contemporary scientific terminology used in the *International Encyclopedia of Psychiatry, Psychology, Psychoanalysis, and Neurology* (1977) the term "morally insane" was replaced by "sociopathic personality."[4]

In 1954, Judge David L. Bazelon of the U.S. Court of Appeals for the District of Columbia issued the *Durham decision*. The Durham decision stated "that an accused is not criminally responsible if his unlawful act was the product of mental disease or defect." Obviously the Durham rule recommended that sociopaths be declared innocent and, as such, acquitted.

In 1972 the District of Columbia revoked the Durham rule and introduced the *Brawner rule* which reads: "A person is not responsible for criminal conduct if at the time of such conduct as a result of mental disease or defect he lacks substantial capacity either to appreciate the criminality of his conduct or to conform his conduct to the requirements of the laws."

The Brawner rule has been accepted with modifications by federal circuit courts and many states, but did not put an end to the controversy. Lawyers, psychiatrists, and psychologists continued to interpret the law in more than one way. The issues of "diminished capacity" and "liberal versus harsh interpretation" have often resulted in "battles of the experts" in court.

One of the most controversial issues is the distinction between *total unawareness of one's actions and the "lack of knowledge of right and wrong."* Psychiatrists have often been asked in court whether the defendant would have committed the crime if faced by an armed policeman. The answer is: In a vast majority of cases a sociopath would not have committed the crime.

Several years ago I founded the International Organization for the Study of Group Tensions. I have written several works about moral principles and their violation via hostility, prejudice, and violence. It seems that the human race is heading toward a catastrophe. The proliferation of violence and of terrorist groups who take the law into their hands, and in the name of some ideals perpetrate hideous crimes against humanity, bears witness to a severe decline of moral standards. We may be going through a period of a suicidal anticulture, and the spread of violent behavior may be just an alarm signal of a growing danger of atomic and hydrogenic war that could put an end to the human race. *Morality is not a luxury. It is a necessity. Without it we may all perish.* What should we do? There are three methods of combating violence and perhaps even preventing it. *The first method is to make it futile.* Terrorist gangs thrive on whatever success they may have. It is the moral obligation of humanity to make them fail. They must not be allowed to get away with their self-righteous violence. They must not be allowed to hijack, kidnap, and murder. The futility of terrorism will put an end to its attractiveness. Failure does not attract sociopaths and futile efforts discourage further efforts.

The first, the short-range method of preventing violence, is to make it futile. The second, the medium-range method, deals with public opinion, and the third, the long-range method, is related to our educational system. Political leaders, intellectuals, and clergymen who, out of sympathy with the political goals of a particular terrorist group, refuse to condemn violence are unaware of the fact that they themselves are responsible *for the destruction of our social and political system and with it, our very civilization.*

Civilization started when wise men imposed rules on social behavior to make life better for all. If we allow some people to act in an uninhibited manner, we might become slaves to a Hitler, a Stalin, a Khomeini, or to anyone else no matter what the slogans are.

Democracy started with a social contract—an agreement that all of us are equal under the law and no one will be allowed to take the law into his or her own hands. People voluntarily renounced the use of power and agreed to obey elected or recognized leaders and judges. Our forefathers created this sociopolitical system and we must protect it and defend it. This system may need amendments or even far-reaching changes, but these changes must be attained in a peaceful and democratic manner. Some revolutionaries may have good ideas, and we may be willing to listen to their *words*, but we must defend ourselves against being massacred by their *swords* and forced to surrender our ideals to theirs.

Prevention of violent behavior hinges on developing a universal public opinion against *all acts of violence*, irrespective of their goals. Humanity must declare that assassins are assassins no matter what their motives. Whether one kills for money or for prejudice or in the name of nationalism or socialism or any other "ism"—he or she is a murderer.

The self-styled idea of elitism must be counteracted by a universal repudiation and condemnation of violence. Newspapers and other mass media must deprive terrorists of their self-styled halo of martyrdom. When a great power trains terrorists, it becomes a party to an undeclared war against civilization.

Moral Education

I repeat, three methods can be used to prevent terrorism: Making it futile, mobilizing public opinion to withdraw support for terrorist groups, and revising our educational system to teach children moral behavior.

The fact that so many young people turn to drugs and/or violence is a dangerous signal. It is easy to blame them, while the responsibility rests with us, the adult society, their parents and teachers. Many adults have forsaken the traditional values and have given their children nothing to hold on to. Today many young people rebel against the *nothingness* of their home life. They seek escape in hippism and drugs, fostering and perpetuating the anticulture of their parents. Under the disguise of liberalism, parents and teachers have abdicated their responsibilities, forgetting that the task of education is not to please the children, but to help them to become responsible adults.

History has shown us a great many instances when abnormal individuals incited destructive wars in the name of lofty ideals. Many bloody wars and massacres of innocent people have been initiated by gifted but disturbed fanatics who, in the name of whatever ideals they professed, sacrificed thousands of human lives.

Hitler, Himmler, Eichmann, Dzierzynski, Stalin, and Beria professed to kill people in the name of some fanatical beliefs. Young people are usually more prone to embrace radical ideas and may therefore fall prey to unscrupulous fanatics and their demagogic methods.

Viewed from a *cultural-historical point of view* social and political dissatisfaction is a positive phenomenon. No society and no generation has found final solutions to problems that perplex humanity, and every effort to review old approaches and to try new methods should be welcome. The trouble lies, therefore, not in the traditional rebellions against tradition, but in the disruptive nature of present-day rebellions that practice violence. Radical slogans do not necessarily represent justice, and forces of brutality, once unleashed, follow their own logic of destruction.

We can prevent violent behavior if we really want to. We must become aware of the threat to humanity and of the possibility that some daring terrorists could get hold of nuclear weapons. Cutting the branches will not solve the problem; we must cut the roots and prevent self-righteous gang leaders from attracting alienated and disenchanted youth.

We must rediscover moral ideals and share them with our children. We must revive the spirit of respect for human life; life is a gift that need not be wasted. We must give the followers and the would-be followers of gang leaders positive goals and a constructive purpose in life. We must inspire young people to try to solve conflicts by negotiations rather than violence. We must teach them that humanity cannot tolerate the Nazi-type "all freedom for some." They must be taught that all people have the same rights, and no one has the right to impose his or her will upon others. We must guide them to work for humanity instead of fighting against it.

Notes

1. J. J. Dilutio Jr., "Crime in America, It's Going to Get Worse," in *Reader's Digest* (August 1995): 55–58.

2. Bertrand Russell, *Power: A New Social Analysis* (New York: W. W. Norton & Co., 1947).

3. James C. Pritchard, *Treatise on Insanity* (London: Gilbert and Piper, 1835).

4. Benjamin B. Wolman, ed., *International Encyclopedia of Psychiatry, Psychology, Psychoanalysis, and Neurology* (New York: Van Nostrand Reinhold and Aesculapius Publishers, 1977).

7

What We Can Do: Moral Education

As explained in chapter 6, several factors contribute to the rise of sociopaths. The decline of parental and school discipline is the leading contributing factor to the spread of sociopathic behavior and the danger of a sociopathic epidemic.

Although genetic factors could possibly be responsible for a fraction of cases, *the vast majority of sociopaths are not born sociopaths.* Children who are exposed to parental neglect and/or abuse and children who witness interparental violence turn sociopathic. Inadequate guidance, lack of moral encouragement, and frequent exposure to pathological selfishness foster sociopathic personality development.

Our society pays a high price for child neglect and abuse, whether it takes place inside or outside the family. Parental neglect, rejection, and hostility wreak havoc with the child's personality. Antisocial behavior and delinquency are most often the result of insufficiency and/or distortions of parental care. Sociopathic behavior is a product of widespread misunderstanding of what education is about. Education must start with *discipline* imposed by parents and teachers, which should help the children to develop self-discipline.

Education and Discipline

Human beings are born helpless and must go through a prolonged developmental process. They cannot grow up by themselves; they need a considerable amount of help. if left alone, they would perish.

Physical care secures survival. *Restraint and guidance are prerequisites for the development of a healthy personality.* Lack of guidance in childhood fosters infantile fixations and immaturity, and causes serious maladjustment. Education must provide the necessary direction and guidance to ensure the attainment of maturity.

Many parents live in a state of utter confusion. Gross misinterpretations of Sigmund Freud and John Dewey, who were opposed to Victorian prudishness and Prussian tyranny, have greatly contributed to a pendular policy swing in the opposite direction. The present-day parental permissiveness borders on abdication of parental rights and responsibilities. Contemporary parents often renounce their social role as adults and parents, and surrender to the whims of their children. Instead of guiding their children, many parents bribe them; instead of setting moral standards, they accept their children's innate lack of morality. Books and

articles written by people who read Freud upside down rec-
ommend that parents speak baby talk and negotiate with
children as equals rather than offer positive and firm
parental guidance.

Parents and children do not share equal rights or equal
responsibilities. Parents must make decisions and they
cannot shun their responsibility. When parents are indecisive, children may sense weakness and assume dictatorial
posture. In many American families the entire household
revolves around a disturbed child who reigns self-destruc-
tive tyranny over his or her parents. Overanxious and over-
solicitous parental attitudes confuse children, destroy their
feeling of security, and disorient them in regard to their
place in the family and in society at large. Excessive
parental "liberalism" does not prepare children for future
adult responsibilities.

Parents have rights. The fact that they have children
must not herald the end of their right to live their own lives.
Parents owe their children love and guidance, but they need
not play the martyr to their children's demands. Children
detest weak parents and do not respect parents who fail to
act as mature adults. Parents must elicit *love and respect*
from their children. Love is not enough; children who don't
respect their parents are unable to develop a correct perception of reality. *Children who were never constrained will
never develop self-restraint.* When they reach adult years,
they will not be prepared for responsible citizenship in a
civilized society. *Education must move from discipline
imposed from without toward self-discipline.*

In early human history parents taught their children a

trade. In due time the children ceased to be dependent upon their parents and were ready to support themselves. This was and is the aim of all schools in all societies. The complex socioeconomic structure of modern times requires a prolonged and complex schooling process. Parents cannot offer such training and they cannot rule the schools. Society at large hires trained experts and bestows on them the responsibility of education, which must help children to outgrow infantile *dependence* and become mature individuals prepared to take part in the *interdependent* network of modern life.

Education cannot be free nor can it give the same rights to parents and children. The so-called free education is not education at all. All democratic societies have instituted *compulsory and authoritarian education.* The aim of schools in a democratic society is to *prepare* children to live in democracy, for a democratic life requires that its members *earn their living and respect the rights of others*.

In order to attain this goal, democratic societies *force* all children to receive proper education, for democracy without public and general education is a mockery. Uneducated people *become a burden* and can easily become either exploited or exploitive.

Education is based on the authority of educators, but even the teachers are not free to do as they please; they *obey* their principals, who *obey* the superintendents, and the entire school administration *obeys* duly elected city, state, and national governments. Democracy does not mean anarchy, but a *willing acceptance of rules and regulations decided upon by the entire society.*

Should children be excluded from this system and allowed to do as they please? Should children decide whether to study and, if so, what to study? Should children decide in matters of spelling, arithmetic, science, classroom behavior, and human relations? Government by children inevitably ends up in a tyranny of a couple of bullies. A permissive school system where teachers do not exercise their authority vested in them by a democratic society leads to a gross abuse of freedom by some children.

Teachers are in school to instruct, and they must teach not what children would like to be taught, but *what the society finds necessary as a preparation for its future members*. Teachers must *control* their classes or they cannot teach; teachers must give tests and evaluate children's progress to be able to offer constructive guidance. Teachers are responsible for preparing children for mature and responsible citizenship.

There is always room for improvement of educational methods and classroom relations, but discipline is a prerequisite for a friendly classroom atmosphere. The "blackboard jungle" that spreads like wildfire throughout the schools of the nation may destroy the nation. *The "blackboard jungle" destroys blackboards and turns schools into jungles.*

College Education

College and university students are on the threshold of adulthood. As students, they must receive guidance from their professors in the respective fields of competence, but students cannot decide what should and what should not be taught in biology, nuclear physics, neurosurgery, business management, or clinical psychology. They are not competent, and they must be taught by those who know.

College and university students are not children. The transition from childhood dependence into adult responsibility must start gradually. Students, as young adults, should be given a voice regarding their future life. They should be informed and consulted, and participate, within reason, in the governing of their colleges. However, they must not lose sight of the fact that they are neither the owners nor the rulers of higher education. Society at large, through its duly elected government, controls public institutions. Colleges and universities belong to the society and not to student groups.

Student groups may dissent, but violence is a crime no matter who practices it. Police cannot solve social and political controversies, but college administrators and educators who permit dissident groups to disrupt the educational process are partners to sociopathic self-righteous behavior. An ill-conceived, irresponsible permissiveness encourages college students to take the law into their own hands, and may lead to a growing chaos in an area where people should be educated to obey the laws and respect the rights of others.

Education means discipline imposed by educators—and it should help children to develop self-discipline and moral responsibility.

America's educational system carries the stigma of *pedocentrism*, that is of bending to the true or imaginary "needs" of children. American children are expected to "express themselves," and their parents and teachers are supposed to listen to the alleged spontaneity of the younger generation. The pedocentric setting of the child in the center of the educational process violates the basic principles of education. Education geared solely to the needs of the child ignores the true nature of childhood. Children are not a distinct species, race, or gender; they represent an early stage of manhood and womanhood. *Children have specific needs related to their age, but the chief need of children is to be helped to cease to be children and to become adults.* Children must not be rushed too early into adulthood, but many parents prevent their children from ever becoming adults.

A gardener who neglects his or her garden must not hide behind a smokescreen of laissez-fairism and liberalism; he or she has simply neglected a duty. Parents who "let their children grow"; who allow the children to do as they please; who instead of helping the children acquire adult patterns of speech and action descend to the children's level, talk baby talk, and act in an infantile manner; are doing a disservice to their children. *Helping a child does not mean helping the child to remain childish.* Infants function on the "pleasure principle" and demand immediate satisfaction of their fancy. Adults who bribe their children instead of educating them are responsible for the epidemic of sociopathy.

Defining Education

It is not customary to discuss education in books dealing with psychology, sociology, and other behavioral sciences.

The reasons are quite obvious. Behavioral sciences are empirical and descriptive and they operate with true or false statements, describing "what is." There are, however, scientific disciplines that determine "what should be." Education is one of those disciplines that sets goals (telos) and proposes ways and means (techniques) for their achievement.

How can a science answer the question "What should be done?" Who sets goals in education? Apparently, the statements of the educational science do not belong to the category of true or false statements. Such statements as, for instance, "Education *should* be compulsory," do not convey empirical knowledge. They are normative, teleological, goal-setting statements.

This normative goal-setting way of reasoning cannot be proven or disproven by scientific inquiry. Small wonder that the history of educational ideas is largely a series of anecdotal stories of what a certain thinker, such as Rousseau, Pestalozzi, Froebel, Herbart, and Dewey decided to set up as a goal for the upbringing of children. Certain goals have been chosen at will, though fad, fashion, and whim still prevail in this large and vital area of human life.

Fads and fashion change, and the history of American education is a case in point. For a long time education was dominated by Herbart's arbitrary and metaphysical system. For a while, Spencer's utilitarianism was the gospel; then Dewey defended the rights of the child to "express himself," while most children had nothing to express. For a while the "core curriculum" dominated the picture; then "Johnny could not read." With every new book and newspaper article the shaky foundations of educational philosophy were torn down and educators embarked on never-ending discussions that could not prove anything.

The Study of Aims

Obviously, science cannot set goals for human activities. Science has to study what is, what *has* been done, but it cannot decide what *should* be done. However, scientific methods can help people to make decisions. Individuals must decide what should be done; society must set norms and aims. Why should we not be helped by an exact knowledge of the prevailing conditions in deciding what should be done in particular circumstances? Is it impossible to convert the search for goals to *research into reasons why people choose a given goal*?

What can be studied is *how people evaluate, judge,* and *decide*. The so-called values, moral principles, and social norms are a *generalization of human attitudes*. The *objectified attitude* of human beings, the *objectified feeling of a society about itself* are the roots of ethics and other principles.

This reasoning brings a far-reaching change in the study of educational goals. We are not asking what the educational goal should be, but what kind of goal can be set to reach this desired outcome. The "should-do" studies do not set aims, but through investigation of the *causes* that led to the setting of aims, they promote the setting of aims. If we know the reasons for setting the aims, we will know what aims have to be set.

Usually people make their choices in accordance with

their *needs*. Individual needs may be contradictory and sub-jective, but social groups *objectify* those needs, generalize them, and then set up norms and define values. These norms, values, and aims originate in the *needs of the respective society*. Those *socially approved needs are the reasons for the goals established by a society*.

For every society this question can be reasonably answered. A society educates the younger generation to join the existing institutions, to support them, and to satisfy the social needs. *Every society establishes its educational ends in accordance with its needs*. The question of "what should be" is converted into a *causal* inquiry: what are the causes that motivate a given society to choose particular educational goals and methods?

Education is not only a social function; it is a biological process. All parents wish to see their children mature socially and biologically. A child is *growing* as well as *learning*. Adults have always tried to assist in this natural development, and this aim, to support the natural process of growing, is the common, unchangeable, eternal aim of education. This is the eternal, *immanent* goal of education: the educational activity in support of the *biological* process of growing.

Societies differ from one another and they attach different meanings to maturity. To be a well-adjusted adult does not mean the same for all societies. The universal goal of education aims at maturity; this is the common, unchangeable goal of education, however one defines maturity. But the social structure and cultural attitudes of different societies are widely divergent. This is the *changing, specific, transcendent* aim of education, different in different times and places.

This brings us to a detailed *descriptive* study of the social forces, economic relations, cultural features, and needs and trends in a *given society.* The educational achievements should satisfy the needs of a given society. This is the *educational criterion*, the *objective measure* of educational achievements.

It is understandable that religious groups, private citizens, and any other factions in American society have the right to develop educational systems according to their particular needs and aims, but the public educational systems supported by the taxes paid by all citizens should serve the broadest needs of our democratic society.

Parents and teachers fulfill their duty in respect to the educational goals as long as they help children to grow physically and intellectually. But they fail in moral aspects of education if they do not help the children to become *adults* capable of assuming responsibility for their future families toward society at large.

It is not enough to "take care" of children and supply them with food, clothing, pocket money, books, skills, and knowledge. All these supplies are necessary for the child's growth, but the child will never become an adult unless he or she is taught to *take care of others.*

Our society must teach each new generation to carry on the role of cooperation, mutual understanding, and helping each other. Education should propagate *social adjustment and moral behavior.*

As we've learned, every human being is born both a

hater and a lover, and which force will motivate behavior depends upon *interaction* with one's environment, especially in the formative years. The newborn's defensive attitude is directed against the external world in a well-justified sense of self-protection. Amoral behavior in adulthood indicates a fixation on or a regression to the newborn stage of total care for oneself excluding everyone else, combined with an offensive-defensive attitude toward others.

Birth does not change the parasitic attitude of the as yet unborn fetus. Although the newborn uses his or her own respiratory system, the parasitic-dependent attitude continues. Infants follow instant stimuli and impulses and operate on the principle of immediate gratification of needs, which Freud dubbed *Lustprinzip*. Infants are therefore *anomous*— amoral and selfish.

Morality means concern for fellow human beings and it starts with restraints imposed from without. Fear of retaliation and punishment is the first small step children take toward moral behavior. The earliest restraints and rules are based on fear, thus the earliest phase of primitive morality should be called *phobonomous*. With the development of rudimentary awareness of potential consequences, called by Freud "archaic ego," the child's selfishness faces restraints. The child learns to obey because he or she fears. Fear is not morality, but primitive people and toddlers must be restrained from without; such restraint breaks the ground for the more advanced phases of morality.

As children become aware of parental love and care, they appreciate what they get and begin to reciprocate. Childhood "love" is quite selfish, for children love only those who love them. The child needs parental love, and fears that he or she may lose it. The child's attitude toward its parents is a combination of love and fear. The child willingly and fearfully accepts parental rules and prohibitions, gradually absorbs these rules, and perceives them as if they were his or her own. The child may identify with the parents or parental substitutes and incorporate their prohibitions and norms. The youngster may engage in self-blame himself or herself for occasional disobedience and develop *guilt feelings* whenever parental rules are violated. Then behavior is *heteronomous*, for children willingly obey norms instituted by others who they perceive as loving and powerful authority figures.

Moral maturity does not reach full development with childhood acceptance of parental rules. Preadolescents and adolescents develop close interpersonal relations with their peers; they form groups, cliques, and gangs. Quite often these new social relations become more powerful than the child-parent attachment, and the rules of peer society become the ultimate source of moral or antimoral behavior. The identification with the peer group to which one chooses to belong may guide one's behavior for years to come. The willing acceptance of social norms, be it of a certain religious denomination, racial or ethnic group, or a political party leads to the formation of a new part of one's personality, and the group identification leads to the *socionomous morality*, that is, acceptance of socially shared norms.

Many people tend to abide by the rather limited moral rules of their particular group. They are "brothers" and "sisters" who share limited moral principles within their brotherhood or sisterhood.

Democratic systems are an outgrowth of a series of agreements; they are socionomous. These agreements are both *voluntary and binding*. They are (1) *voluntary*, for whoever does not approve of the existing laws is free to leave the country and seek refuge elsewhere. They are, however, (2) *binding* for whoever lives in the territory where these rules are accepted. They are usually written down as a code of law that often includes a national constitution. Democratic systems provide for (3) *equal rights* and *equal obligations* for all citizens, that is, the same degree of freedom for all, and not all freedom for some. (4) The binding decisions, laws, and regulations are arrived at and determined by *majority rule*. Democratic systems provide for freedom of speech that enables the minority to argue its cause and eventually become integrated into the majority. (5) The governing bodies are *elected* by *free elections* in which all citizens can vote for whomever they please. (6) Last, but certainly not least, democracy is based on a voluntary and binding renunciation of violence. A judicial system is established and adversaries present their case to an impartial court whose decisions are binding.

There are no perfect democratic systems and violent acts cannot be totally eradicated. However, democracy has significantly contributed to a reduction of self-righteous and violent behavior; and although the legal and judicial systems require strengthening and improvements, the vast majority of people in democratic countries abide by the law and refrain from self-righteous acts and violence.

Nothing of that sort took place in international relations. International relations are still governed by lawlessness, greed, paranoid fears, overemphasis on national pride, and total disinhibition. Under the disguise of diplomacy and legalistic deals, most governments led by megalomaniacs and other irresponsible individuals are ready to plunge humanity into a bloody catastrophe.

The Need for Restraint from Within

Moral behavior must be acquired since it is not innate. A newborn child reacts violently to restraints from without but it is unable to restrain itself. Every human being is born with the inclination to fight for survival, that is, with a narcissistic, self-directed libido and a self-defensive, object-directed destrudo. As described earlier, there are four distinct phases in moral development, starting with a total lack of morality, the *anomous-id* phase, followed by the *phobonomous* phase where self-restraint is based on fear, through the *heteronomous* phase, when a combination of fear and love leads to identification with the peer group, and ultimately to the self-imposed *autonomous* phase of moral behavior.

The highest level of moral development has been exemplified in Ibsen's play *An Enemy of the People*, when an individual accepts moral responsibility even when he or she does so alone. This is the highest *autonomous* level of morality. It is the irrevocable moral commitment of an individual.

At all developmental phases, parents and teachers must

comply with the biological, immanent goal of education in fostering natural growth and development. The methods of education must be adjusted to each particular developmental phase. Moral education starts at home. It starts at the first level of anomy, goes through the second fear-based phase of moral formation, followed by heteronomy in which fear is tempered with love, and continues through the phase of the socionomous development. As children grow, they must assume more and more responsibility. Children who were never taught moral behavior and were never helped in their development can become sociopaths. Moral education can prevent sociopathic epidemics.

Responsibility that is too heavy and occurs too early in life can be discouraging, but the lack of responsibility can turn children into selfish sociopathic individuals.[1] Growing sons and daughters must learn to share the responsibility for the family. When they leave home and start their own family, they will be ready to assume responsibility for their spouses and children.

Self-Education and Self-Discipline

The final phase of every educational process is self-education. Only we can teach ourselves to have the courage to give. One reaches the highest moral level when one does not expect approval or reward for good deeds. One is a *free human being* when one acts in accordance with one's own *reason* and *conscience*, and reaches a harmony between what one believes is rational and what is moral. Every new situation calls for new decisions, which should be made without depending on parental or societal approval.

Self-education is a never-ending process, and its ultimate goal is the understanding that there is no escape from death, but life must be lived to its fullest by *becoming more human through becoming more humane.*

While one cannot assume that education and self-education are blocked by television, it is equally difficult to ignore the negative impact of what children see on the screen every day. Marc Silver writes:

> To hell with kids—that must be the motto of the new fall TV series. You want proof? Look at the network lineups. Many of the wholesome sitcoms that once ruled the 8 P.M.-to-9 P.M. hour have gone to the TV graveyard, replaced by racier fare like *Cybill* and *Roseanne*. As a *Wall Street Journal* news story put it in a recent headline, "It's 8 P.M. Your Kids Are Watching Sex on TV." . . .
>
> Say goodbye to the "family hour," the 8 P.M.-to-9 P.M. period ABC, CBS, and NBC once reserved for you and the kids, and say hello to the Fox in the henhouse. The success of sexually frank programs like the Fox network's *Beverly Hills 90210* at 8 P.M. has uncorked a wave of me-tooism in the quest for a young (but not too young), hip and urban audience. As Alan Sternfeld, an ABC senior vice president, says of shifting *Roseanne* and *Ellen* to 8 P.M.: "We get reimbursed by advertisers when we deliver adults 18 to 49."[2]

Certainly TV is hardly contributing much to moral education, and some television programs contribute to the rise of sociopaths and the danger of an epidemic.

Notes

1. Benjamin B. Wolman, *The Sociopathic Personality* (New York: Brunner Mazel, 1987).

2. Marc Silver, "Sex and Violence on TV," *U.S. News & World Report*, September 11, 1995, p. 62.

8

Educational
Perspectives

Biosocial Perspectives

Lower biological species do not need education; a "newborn" protozoan is as "mature" as an adult one. Maturity implies the ability to face life, including the ability to fight for survival and to be reasonably adjusted to one's environment.

Birds need some "education" since they are not mature at the start of their lives. They must grow and learn, and reach the stage where they don't need parental care and can leave the nest.

The higher the biological species, the longer the road from the beginning of life to maturity. Newborn human infants need a prolonged period of protection and care. Infants cannot survive without someone supplying food and shelter, and offering adequate protection against hunger, bad weather, and enemies. The neonate human is helpless.

Children have no say in choosing the environment that influences their opportunities. Adults have some degree of mobility; they can change jobs, places of residence, marital relations, religion, business associations, or political affiliation. Children are born to and brought up by people they did not choose, and they are, indeed, a captive audience in their parents' homes.

Adults can create a more or less stable environment as they choose. Excluding major catastrophes, such as earthquakes and wars, adults can live all their years in a certain neighborhood, practice a certain occupation, develop friendly relations with business associates and relatives, and establish structured daily routines. Children do not have these options. They must move to a new neighborhood and attend a new school whenever their parents decide to, and they must accept a new, and in some cases unfriendly, physical and social environment not of their choice. Children may feel uprooted whenever their parents decide to change their place of residence, their family relationships, or any other social contacts.

Adults remain adult as long as they live, whether they are young or middle-aged or old, and their behavior patterns are more or less circumscribed by their sex, age, occupation, and religion. Children's behavioral patterns are continuously changing. *No child is allowed to remain a child, and no child is allowed to be an adult.* Growth and maturation are processes of change, and the terms of change are arbitrarily and often whimsically determined by their parents.

Children have very little power of their own, and their parents have all the power to promote or destroy their mental health. A self-confident person reacts to a danger by mobilizing resources, but rejection, isolation, and abandonment adversely affect a child who has very little self-confidence and practically no self-reliance.

Traumatized, hurt, and anxious children may *regress* to an earlier phase of development where they might feel better protected and more secure. A kindergarten-age child may regress to baby talk, and a school-age child may become a bed wetter.

Mature adults *first* count on themselves and *then* on their friends, relatives, and others. Children must count on others, on the loving and protecting parents or parental substitutes. *An adult's security depends on power first and acceptance second; a child's security depends on acceptance by others first and personal power next.* Power has been defined as the ability to satisfy needs, and survival is all encompassing and universal. Acceptance has been defined as the willingness to satisfy the needs of other people by helping and protecting them.

The presence of loving parents or parental substitutes is necessary for a child's mental health and development into a well-adjusted adult. Children need help in the process of growing up and reaching maturity. They must grow stronger and wiser and develop a realistic estimate of their physical and mental resources. They need help and encouragement in the natural process of shifting from depending on others to a growing sense of self-reliance.

Children gradually develop the ability for reality testing. They learn and mature gradually, and every child has his/her own biologically determined speed of maturation and innate ability to learn and profit from experience. Parents can provide opportunities for growth.

Parental Care

The belief in a universal and innate inclination of parental care was never proven, although several species, such as birds and mammals, usually do take care of their children. Parental care includes supplying food, protection against enemies, and training that prepares the offspring to become a self-reliant adult.

In ancient societies parents exercised total control over their children. In most modern societies child care is regulated by laws that safeguard children's rights. As mentioned above, the very survival of a newborn human child depends totally on the protection received from parents or parental substitutes. The physical and mental development of children is greatly influenced by the care they receive. Although some mental traits are genetically determined, even the best seed cannot develop in acid fluid, and the child's innate potentialities need a favorable environment.

Lack of adequate maternal care can inhibit children's mental development. During World War II Anna Freud and Dorothy Burlingham studied children sent away from London under the Blitz to safety in the country. Children who stayed with their parents in London were emotionally better off than those who were sent away. Separation from parents causes harm to children's mental health.

A positive and encouraging parental attitude contributes

to children's appropriate behavior and reduces the instances of inappropriate behavior. An affectionate attitude toward a child, parental acceptance of the child the way the child is, and positive reinforcement of the child's behavior greatly contribute to a wholesome personality development. Children brought up by rational and caring parents tend to develop a positive attitude to themselves and others. Parental acceptance and reinforcement of the child's learning has a significant effect on the child's intellectual development, and an affectionate interaction between the father and the mother greatly contributes to the children's behavior in their future marriage and family life. However, intraparental strife adversely affects the child's personality. Some divorced parents use their children as a captive audience by inciting them against the other parent, thus implicating children in problems of adult life.

Some parents unwillingly and unwittingly cause harm to their children's mental health. Parental overprotection infantilizes the children, undermines their self-confidence, and makes them feel inadequate. An inconsistent parental attitude of rejecting the child and showering it with affection when the child is ill or badly hurt teaches the child a masochistic lesson that defeat of pain is the only way to gain acceptance and love. Overdemanding parents make the children feel guilty for not being able to live up to their standards: the children resent themselves for being inadequate and their parents for asking for too much. Parental indifference and outright rejection leads children to develop exceeding selfishness and hostile behavior.

Sociocultural Perspectives

Education is the carrier of civilization. One can easily imagine what could have happened to humankind without education. Education carries the human race up from the caves to civilized life.

Whatever we have, all achievements in all aspects of life, our economy, our houses, our communication—all this is transmitted by education. There would be no paved roads, no cooked food, no houses built, and no art and no science without education. There would be no medical care, no hospitals, no doctors, no nurses, and disease would decimate the population. Whatever people would create in art and science would die with the creators.

The very survival of the human race depends on learning to cooperate. Education teaches people to cooperate.

Can Violence Be Controlled?

In 1932 Sigmund Freud expressed a pessimistic view in a reply to one of Albert Einstein's letters:

> So what when human beings are incited to war they may have a whole number of motives. . . . There is no need to enumerate them all. A lust for aggression and destruction is certainly among them: The countless cruelties in history and in our everyday lives vouch for its existence and its strength. . . . When we read of the atrocities of the past, it sometimes seems as though the idealistic motives served only as an excuse for the destructive appetites;

and sometimes—as in the case, for instance, of the cruelties of the Inquisition—it seems as though the idealistic motives had pushed themselves forward into consciousness, while the destructive ones lent themselves an unconscious reinforcement.

It is a general principle, then, that conflicts of interests between men are settled by the use of violence. This is true of the whole animal kingdom, from which men have no business to exclude themselves.

There is no use in trying to get rid of men's aggressive inclinations. If the destructive forces turn inwardly, they are suicidal. When they are used for destruction of the external world, this brings inner relief. This would serve as a biological justification for all the ugly and dangerous impulses against which we are struggling.[1]

Freud believed that a community is held together by two things: the compelling forces of violence and the emotional ties (identification is the technical name) between its members. No community can tolerate a war of all against all and, in order to survive, it must establish peace among its members. Wars could be prevented by creating a supreme authority, for the force of a group can prevent violence by individuals. A League of Nations could prevent war among nations if such a league had the power of a superstate above the nation-states.

Freud believed that unity through love or identification is another method for preventing war. Brotherhoods in faith can prevent wars amongst the brothers but not against outsiders.

The limitation of aggression is the first and perhaps the

hardest sacrifice which society demands from each individual. We have learned in what an ingenious way this
unruly element is tamed. The setting up of the superego,
which makes the dangerous, aggressive impulses its own,
is like introducing a garrison into a province that is on the
brink of rebellion. The ego does not feel at all comfort-
able when it finds itself sacrificed in this way to the needs
of society, when it has to submit itself to the destructive
impulses of aggression, which it would have dearly liked
to have set in motion against others. It is like carrying
over into the region of the mind the dilemma—eat or to
be eaten—which dominated the organic world. Fortunately the instincts of aggression are never alone, they are
always alloyed with the erotic ones. In the cultural conditions which man has created for himself, the erotic
instincts have much to mitigate and much to avert.[2]

A newborn human being has no moral principles whatsoever. They are driven by unconscious, impulsive forces of
Ares and Eros, both of them aiming at their own survival. A
hungry infant sucks his thumb or her mother's breasts, irrespective of her health or well-being. Neonates are selfish
and amoral. They need to be educated to cooperate with
others.

Education Starts at Home

The present crisis in education is a crisis of parents and
teachers who, being themselves immature, refuse to assume
responsibility toward their children, hide behind clichés, or
follow stereotyped advice from books, newspapers, or televi-

sion programs. There is, however, no substitute for parental effort toward self-understanding and an understanding of their particular child. But education is not foolproof.

At the present time, "freedom" is in vogue. People who have read Freud's books upside down preach "educational liberalism," as if complete freedom were the true objective of education, and restraint were a threat to a child's normal development.

The idea of freedom in education borders on sheer nonsense. Every child is born with a load of impulses (the id), but if he or she is allowed to remain an infant and act on impulse, no child will ever become a normal adult.

Education does not mean pleasing or bribing children. Education is a process that aims at helping children become mature individuals. A mature individual assumes responsibility for his or her behavior within an occupation, a family life, and in the community at large.

A mature adult is not "free"; he or she accepts commitments and honors them. Only infants, dictators, and raving maniacs demand unlimited freedom for themselves with no consideration for other people. Democracy means equal rights for all. Sociopaths demand all rights for themselves.

Notes

1. Freud 1932, p. 383.
2. Freud 1933, pp. 151–52.

Bibliography

Adler, Leonard L., and Florence L. Denmark, eds. *Violence and the Prevention of Violence.* Westport, Conn.: Praeger, 1995.

American Psychiatric Association. *Diagnostic and Statistical Manual of Mental Disorders.* 3d ed., rev. Washington, D.C., 1987.

————. *Violence and Youth: Psychology's Response.* Washington, D.C., 1993.

Andreopoulos, G., ed. *Conceptual and Historical Dimensions of Genocide.* Philadelphia: University of Pennsylvania Press, 1994.

Bandura, Albert. *Aggression: A Social Learning Analysis.* Englewood Cliffs, N.J.: Prentice Hall, 1973.

Baron, R. A. *Human Aggression.* New York: Plenum, 1977.

Beer, Francis A. *Peace Against War: The Ecology of International Violence.* San Francisco: W. H. Freeman, 1981.

Buber, Martin. *I and Thou.* Translated by Ronald Gregor Smith. New York: Scribners, 1958.

Burke, Kenneth. *On Symbols and Society.* Chicago: University of Chicago Press, 1969.

Camus, Albert. *The Myth of Sisyphus*. New York: Philosophical Library, 1956.

Charny, I. W. "Toward a Generic Definition of Genocide." *Conceptual and Historical Dimensions of Genocide,* edited by G. Andreopoulos. Philadelphia: University of Pennsylvania Press, 1984.

Cousins, E. "Many-Leveled Psyche: Correlation Between Psychotherapy and Spiritual Life." *Psychoanalysis and Catholicism*, edited by Benjamin B. Wolman, pp. 31–64. Northvale, N.J.: Jason Aronson, 1995.

Dilutio, J. J., Jr. "Crime in America, It's Going to Get Worse." *Reader's Digest*, August 1995, 55–58.

Eissler, K. R., ed. *Searchlights on Delinquency*. New York: International Universities Press, 1949.

Feshbach, S., and R. Singer. *Television and Aggression*. San Francisco: Jossey-Bass, 1990.

Freud, Sigmund. *An Outline of Psychoanalysis*. New York: Norton, 1979.

Fromm, Erich. *The Sane Society*. New York: Fawcett, 1955.

Goldstein, A., and L. Krasner, eds. *Prevention and Control of Aggression*. New York: Pergamon Press, 1983.

Heidegger, Martin. *Being and Time*. New York: Harper and Row, 1962.

Ibsen, Henrick. *Collected Works of Henrik Ibsen*. N.p.: Oxford University Press, 1906–1912.

Karpman, B., ed. *Symposia on Child and Juvenile Delinquency*. Washington, D.C.: Psychotherapy Monographs, 1959, 143–44.

Kierkegaard, Søren. *Either-Or*. New York: 1843.

Kohlberg, Lawrence. *The Meaning and Measurement of Moral Development*. Clark, Mass.: Clark University Press, 1979.

Kropotkin, Petr. *Mutual Aid: A Factor of Evolution*. Boston: Extending Horizons Books, 1955.

Kupperman, Robert H., and Jeff Kamen. *Final Warning— Averting Disaster in the New Age of Terrorism*. New York: Doubleday, 1989.

Kupperman, Robert H., and Darrell M. Trent. *Terrorism: Threat, Reality, Response*. New York: McGraw Hill, 1977.

Lefer, L. "The Edge of Violence." *Journal of the American Academy of Psychoanalysis* 12 (1984): 253–68.

Lefkowitz, Monroe, et al. *Growing Up to be Violent: A Longitudinal Study of the Development of Aggression*. Elmsford, N.Y.: Pergamon Press, 1977.

Levine, M., R. A. Toro, and D. V. Perkins. "Social and Community Interventions." *Annual Review of Psychology* 44 (1993): 525–58.

Lévi-Strauss, Claude. *Structural Anthropology*. New York: Doubleday, 1967.

Levy, D. M. "The Deprived and Indulged Forms of Psychopathic Personality." *American Journal of Orthopsychiatry* 21 (1950): 250–54.

Lewin, Kurt. *A Dynamic Theory of Personality*. New York: McGraw-Hill, 1933.

Lochlin, J. C., L. W. Willerman, and J. M. Horn. "Human Behavior Genetics." *Annual Review of Psychology* 39 (1988): 101–33.

Lodge, J. ed. *Terrorism: A Challenge to the State*. New York: St. Martin's Press, 1981.

Lombroso, Cesare. *Crime, Its Causes and Remedies*. Translated by Henry P. Horton. Boston: Little, Brown, 1911.

Mosher, D. L., K. E. O'Grady, and H. A. Katz. "Hostility, Guilt, Guilt Over Aggression and Self-Punishment." *Journal of Personality Assessment* 44 (1980): 34–40.

National Victims Center. *Rape in America: A Report to the Nation.* Washington, D.C., 1993.

Pallone, N., and J. Hennessey. *Criminal Behavior: A Process Psychology Analysis.* New Brunswick, N.J.: Transaction Publishers, 1992.

Pritchard, James C. *Treatise on Insanity.* London: Gilbert and Piper, 1835.

Prothrow-Smith, Deborah. *Deadly Consequences.* New York: HarperCollins, 1991.

Reed, John. *Ten Days That Shook the World.* New York: Modern Library, 1935.

Reid, William H., ed. *The Psychopath: A Comprehensive Study of Antisocial Disorders and Behavior.* New York: Brunner-Mazel, 1978.

Rousseau, Jean-Jacques. *The Social Contract and Discourses.* New York: Everyman, 1924.

Russell, Bertrand. *Power: A New Social Analysis.* New York: Norton, 1947.

———. *Philosophy and Politics.* London: 1947.

Sartre, Jean-Paul. *Being and Nothingness.* New York: Philosophical Library, 1956.

Shirer, William L. *The Rise and Fall of the Third Reich.* Greenwich, Conn.: Faucett, 1959–1960.

Silver, Marc. "Sex and Violence on TV." *U.S. News & World Report,* September 11, 1995.

Tharp, R. G., and T. J. Ciborowski, eds. *Perspectives on Cross-Cultural Psychology*. New York: Academic Press, 1979.

Tillich, Paul. *The Courage to Be*. New Haven, Conn.: Yale University Press, 1952.

Wilson, H. "Juvenile Delinquency in Problem Families in Cardiff." *British Journal of Delinquency* 9 (1958): 95–101.

Wolfgang, M. E., R. M. Figlio, and T. Sellin. *Delinquency in a Birth Cohort*. Chicago: University of Chicago Press, 1970.

Wolman, Benjamin B. *Call No Man Normal*. New York: International Universities Press, 1973.

———. *Handbook of Developmental Psychology*. Englewood Cliffs, N.J.: Prentice Hall, 1982.

———. *Logic of Science in Psychoanalysis*. New York: Columbia University Press, 1984.

———. "On Saints, Fanatics, and Dictators." *International Journal of Group Tensions* 4 (1974): 359–84.

———. *Personality Dynamics*. New York: Plenum, 1992.

———. *The Science of Moral Behavior* (in press).

———. *The Sociopathic Personality*. New York: Brunner Mazel, 1987.

Wolman, Benjamin B., ed. *International Encyclopedia of Psychiatry, Psychology, Psychoanalysis and Neurology*. New York: Van Nostrand Reinhold and Aesculapius Publishers, 1977.

———. *Psychoanalytic Interpretation of History*. New York: Basic Books, 1970.

———. *Between Survival and Suicide*. New York: Gardner Press, 1976.

Wolman, Benjamin B., and J. Money, eds. *Handbook of Human Sexuality*. Northvale, N.J.: Jason Aronson, 1994.

Wolman, Benjamin B., and G. Stricker, eds. *Depressive Disorders*. New York: John Wiley & Sons, 1990.

———. *Handbook of Family and Marital Therapy*. New York: Plenum, 1983.

Index